ENTER
EMPTY

HOW LESS IS MORE
WITH GOD

JASON WILSON

ISBN: 978-1-960452-07-8
E-book ISBN: 978-1-960452-08-5
Library of Congress Control Number: 2024917327

Printed in the United States of America.

Endorsements

Jason Wilson is one of the most passionate and authentic pastors I know. In his book *Enter Empty* he brings grace-filled course corrections in how we approach God. If we enter full, we leave empty. But if we enter empty, we always leave full. As you read this life-altering book, you will be empowered to simplify and intensify your focus. It will resource your inner man to go further, reach higher, and dive deeper in your pursuit to be a carrier of the presence of God.

> **Apostle Les Bowling**
> Founder and Apostle of Eagle Rock Covenant Network
> Pastor of Eagle Rock Church

Jason Wilson is a leader among leaders, and having known him for many years alongside my late husband, Bishop Tony Miller, we always believed he had a powerful book waiting to be penned. *Enter Empty* is precisely that book. It emphasizes the importance of making room for God in every season of life. When we come to Him with open hearts, He begins to move in amazing ways. This book reminds us that emptying ourselves is not the conclusion but rather a powerful invitation. It shares not only personal stories and insights, but also profound truths rooted in God's Word. It beautifully illustrates how, as we empty ourselves and pour out for Him, God draws us closer to Himself. *Enter Empty* will surely encourage and uplift you as you journey through its pages of truth.

> **Pastor Kathy Miller**
> Wife of the late Bishop Tony Miller
> President of Destiny Fellowship Network

Jason Wilson has opened his heart to share insights into his life and ministry in *Enter Empty*. From the beginning of his ministry he has followed his passion for more of God's presence. Now, he allows us to be a part of his journey. He started Rejuvenate Church on the premise of seeking God and sharing this message with others. This book contains great insights on how to follow the path of emptying ourselves and how to pursue a lifestyle of being filled with God. It will challenge you to seek the face of God.

Pastor Lane Sargent
Pastor and Evangelist
Former Pastor of Sumiton Church of God

Dedication

THIS BOOK IS, FIRST AND FOREMOST, dedicated to my wife and three children. You are with me in the good and the bad, the pain and the process. You endure the journey that makes the message. And whoever this message may reach and impact to the glory of God, we're doing it together; it's your impact too. I love you more than you can imagine. Our best days are still ahead.

I also want to dedicate this book to every leader, every person, every man and woman of God who find themselves in the wilderness or on the brink of it. Keep walking with Him. He will reveal the promise.

Contents

ACKNOWLEDGEMENTS

I WOULD LIKE TO RECOGNIZE, celebrate, and thank the following people for the part you've played in my life and the vessels you've been to help make this message available.

The Iversen family: You have and continue to be such an enormous vessel of God's goodness in my life and ministry. A heart full of gratitude and a million thanks are not enough. I'm so very grateful.

Bishops Tony (late) and Kathy Miller, Apostles Les and Sheila Bowling, and Pastors Lane and Judy Sargent: I thank God our lives are connected. You all mean so much to me and have such a mark on anything that I am and will become. Thank you for believing in me enough to invest. I'm thankful and humbled. I love you very much.

John Mason and the team at Insight International: For your help in making this book a reality, and really more so, for believing and helping me believe that it should be a reality. I've watched how God has directed many things in our journey together, from the first conversation, through times of collaboration, until now. My prayer is that you have been impacted by our time together, as I have been, by your partnership in the work.

Last, my team, intercessory prayer team, and the family of people at Rejuvenate Church. You believe in what God is doing, you pray for me and my family, and you partner with faith, hope, and love to see the Kingdom of God and His glory revealed in the Earth as it is in Heaven. You were the seedbed for this message, that now we trust will inspire a harvest of revival for many. We are going to change the world together. I love you so much.

CHAPTER 1:

ARE YOU FULL?

HOW FULL IS YOUR LIFE? Family, work, and hobbies. Church. In a fast-paced world full of things to do, people to see, and problems to solve, it's easy to find ourselves with a full schedule . . . and yet wonder at the end of the day if we've accomplished anything.

We fill our lives with work and our kids' activities and try to carve out time for family and friends—and maybe, just maybe, a little downtime. Information is ready to overload us on our TVs, emails, and mobile devices, and always available in our pockets or purses.

When you go to bed at night and try to wind down, or find even the briefest moment to think about it all, does it feel like the things you fill your days with are *meaningful*? Does it all too often feel like empty calories—as though our lives are full of junk food that doesn't really satisfy us? Perhaps you've wondered if God has something else for you, something more meaningful?

Let me assure you, He has much greater promises for His children than we're currently experiencing. I'm going to show you something powerful that changed my world completely! God has something new in store for His people. It's not a new program or event, a church growth strategy, or a life hack.

God has something new for you that will completely change your life if you're open to it, but it's not something *more* that will set you free.

It's something *less*.

Making Room for God

God first put this book on my heart in the form of a sermon right after we emerged from nine long months of fighting the COVID pandemic. I was getting ready to preach on a Sunday morning when I felt God begin to speak to my heart about the upcoming year.

I ONLY CHOOSE EMPTY VESSELS.

It was November 2020, and I was asking God how to open 2021. While sitting in the ready room at church one Sunday morning, about to go out for service, I heard this in my heart, "Tell them to enter empty. Do away with the vision boards, the resolutions, and the plans. It is all a pursuit to attempt to fill their life with something that will help them feel better about themselves; to feel more full or valuable—so many things that aren't Me. I'm sick of full. I only choose empty vessels."

God also said, "You must simplify things. You process more than I ever created and gave you the grace to process. You are inundated with information, and I was to be your only source; the only thing that was to inform you." What informs you, forms you.

As I prayed and studied this revelation, I felt like God began to increase my understanding so I could better see how we have filled our lives with so many worthless *things*. They're not necessarily bad things, like sin, but they're not *Him*. I believe God's will for His people, His church, and for you and me especially, is that we leave it all behind.

Why? To make room for the only One who really matters.

It's pretty common to worry and to think about the things of this world—what we're going to eat, wear, drive, and do. God knows that we need these things and that they're necessary, but He doesn't want us preoccupied with them as the world is preoccupied. He has something better in mind for His people.

Matthew 6:33 tells us, *"But seek first the kingdom of God and His righteousness, and all these things shall be added to you."* We've had it backward. We've been seeking the other things first, with a little bit of God on the side, but He is making it very clear this is not His will for His church or for us individually.

God is about to change the landscape of the church. This book is a prophetic announcement that God has more in store for us than lives filled with the spiritual equivalent of junk food's empty calories. He has prepared a banquet for us (see Luke 14:16-24)—the choice foods are ready, the drinks are poured, and the settings are placed. He has sent out invitations to the usual guests, those who know how to look the part, but they have not accepted. They made their excuses, but they have not surrendered their lives, their programs, and their agendas to Him.

He's done with all that, and now He's drawing in those from the highways and hedges who are hurt, broken, disappointed, and lonely. He wants those with a limp, who have seen great sorrow and sadness, and who are broken in spirit. They've been forgotten, abandoned, and discounted. They don't know how to play the part, but in their brokenness, they have found something many of us are missing—a hunger for God's presence. They often don't even know what they're hungry for, but they know that the things of this world do not satisfy. They have chased the wind and found nothing (see Ecclesiastes 1:14). They know it's all meaningless.

They're beginning to recognize that they are *empty*, and God stands ready to fill them—and us. But He'll only do it if we'll let Him.

WE'VE BECOME A CULTURE OF PERFORMANCE BUT NO PRESENCE.

So, let me ask you, are you hungry for more of God?

Have We Lost Our Way?

This is the story of the church: Each move of God starts out on fire, but we've become preoccupied with our buildings, programs, and content; a culture of performance but no presence. We're giving ourselves over to a myriad of charismatic voices but few that are filled with the Spirit of the Lord. We're busy, yet all this work we're doing misses the heart of God and the invitation to be full of *Him*. So, He's issued the invitation to those who know life's emptiness.

When I shared all of this with my spiritual father, Bishop Tony Miller, he got very excited because God had given him a dream of a great feast prepared on a massive table just the night before. He knew from the dream that things were going to really shift, and that God was done with excuses. As we talked, I began to weep because God had shown me the same things six weeks before, and now He was confirming it through the mouth of a father in the faith.

God is preparing to do a new thing in us and in His church—something unprecedented that we can't measure by yesterday's experiences. God isn't going to do work like Acts 2 again because He has already done it, and it doesn't need to happen again. But I do believe we are in a bookend era. As Acts 2 birthed the church through a pouring out of His Spirit, a seismic outpouring is upon us that will bookend what began in Acts 2 and usher in the eternal reign. It's something greater than we have the ability to comprehend, for the end of a thing is better than its beginning. It's a move that authentically displays the Father, so it must be void of us.

God wants to do something *new*, and it's my prayer that as you read this book, you will catch His vision for your life and for His church. God desires that we set aside our agendas, and the things that preoccupy us, so we may enter His presence empty and ready to be filled *with Him*.

We are Ambassadors

God never intended to do anything on the Earth without us. He created us in His image and likeness to channel His presence. We're ambassadors of the Kingdom of God, so we're His voice in a foreign land. Yet, we do not speak our own opinions; instead, when we authentically represent Him, we speak only the words of our King.

Throughout Scripture, when God prepares to move in the Earth, He doesn't send an event or a system, He sends a person. From Adam and Eve, Noah, Abraham, Moses, all the way to Mary, and the apostles through to today, God has chosen to move through fallible human beings. God even sent His own Son as a Man, and through Him, God transformed the world with the greatest move ever known. Thanks to Him, He doesn't dwell in things or buildings; He lives in people. Your local meeting place is not the church–*you and I* are the church, and we were made to be vessels to hold the most incredible glory imaginable.

But what can you put into a vessel that's already full?

God's will is to show love to humanity, to show His power and authority. He desires to drive out darkness, overcome sickness, heal broken relationships, cure mental disorders, and so much more, but He has chosen to do these things through earthen vessels–*us*.

Beginning a New Season

When I share with people that God wants us to enter empty, I often have to explain a bit more so they can understand, and I tell them how the Lord first laid this on my heart. As I mentioned, I first began to receive this prophetic message for God's people when I was getting ready to walk out to speak at Rejuvenate Church, where I'm the lead pastor. God began to lay the idea on my heart, and eventually, I shared the messages that inspired this book in the context of entering a new year. I want to present it to you in a similar light because I feel like it helps to have a framework. It may not be the start of a year as you read this, but it will be a new start for *you*, whatever season you find yourself in.

The biggest thing I want to get out of the way immediately is that nothing in this book is about us *trying* harder. It's not about us becoming holier by our efforts, willpower, or practices. In fact, that's the polar opposite of God's intention. If we think we can make room for a new move of God through our own efforts, we're right back where we started—filling up with the wrong things. Instead, we're going to see that God is offering us an invitation to be filled by the Holy Spirit's divine power, which we never could accomplish through any of our own efforts.

The idea that we can make ourselves holy, or make promises to God to earn His good favor, is at the root of the religious ideology that has so encumbered the church. We cannot earn the grace and favor of God, no matter how dedicated we are or how pious we sound. Instead, this book will be about the opposite—leaving all of that behind so that a genuine move of God can set us free.

I believe we are on the cusp of something revolutionary. All you need to do is look around to see how desperately this world needs revival! In the last few years, the challenges have increased. Darkness has worked overtime; we need the light. Politicians cannot fix what is wrong with our world, and sadly, neither can many of the programs and policies the organized church has implemented. Like the things we fill our individual lives with, many of these church activities are full of *us* . . . but lacking in *God*.

More programs will not save the world, just like more activities will not make your life feel more complete or satisfying. Only true revival will address the problems destroying our world, and we will only experience revival if we empty ourselves of all the clutter that is filling our vessels so the Lord can fill us with more and more of His Spirit. A move of God will happen through people *just like you*. It cannot happen without a download from Heaven, and that download doesn't happen in a church building. It happens in *you and me*.

> **A MOVE OF GOD WILL HAPPEN THROUGH PEOPLE *JUST LIKE YOU*.**

When we receive this outpouring of the Holy Spirit, we will express the very nature of the love, power, authority, and dominion of God. We will see the Good News proclaimed to the poor, freedom for the prisoners, recovery of sight for the blind, the oppressed set free, and a new move of God on the Earth. A great cloud of witnesses is cheering us on, and if we want to run this race set before us, we must lay aside everything holding us back. God will not share space, and He will not pour His Spirit into unclean vessels.

He is holy and demands holiness of us, as well. I'm so thankful He knows we cannot do this on our own! Let's take a look at His plan for us together, using examples from Scripture. God has a plan for His children, examples we can follow, and He has given us His Holy Spirit to instruct and empower us.

Will you join me and Enter Empty?

CHAPTER 2:

LIVING ON CREDIT

LOOK AROUND YOUR HOUSE. How many of the things you see did you buy on credit? I'm not trying to make a statement about your financial practices, but perhaps you've had the thought, "What if I lost my job?" If you still owe money on the cars in your driveway, your TV, or your house, you can perhaps identify with the fear that one day, if you lost your source, the creditor would come calling. All those things we think of as "ours" actually belong to one bank or another–whoever holds the loan. What happens if the bill comes due, but you cannot pay?

God used the story of a woman in the Bible to teach me about how we enter empty, through her story of this very thing. Her husband had died, and the bills were coming due. The creditor was on the way, and without a miracle, he would take her sons into slavery as payment, leaving her broken, destitute, and alone. So, she turned to God through one of the greatest prophets of the Old Testament, Elisha.

We find her story in 2 Kings 4:1-7, and please bear with me and read the whole passage we'll be exploring:

A certain woman of the wives of the sons of the prophets cried out to Elisha, saying, "Your servant my husband is dead, and you know that your servant feared the Lord. And the creditor is coming to take my two sons to be his slaves."

So Elisha said to her, "What shall I do for you? Tell me, what do you have in the house?" And she said, "Your maidservant has nothing in the house but a jar of oil."

Then he said, "Go, borrow vessels from everywhere, from all your neighbors—empty vessels; do not gather just a few. And when you have come in, you shall shut the door behind you and your sons; then pour it into all those vessels, and set aside the full ones."

So she went from him and shut the door behind her and her sons, who brought the vessels to her; and she poured it out. Now it came to pass, when the vessels were full, that she said to her son, "Bring me another vessel."

And he said to her, "There is not another vessel." So the oil ceased. Then she came and told the man of God. And he said, "Go, sell the oil and pay your debt; and you and your sons live on the rest."

This woman's husband was dead, but God had something great in store for her—something divinely powerful delivered by a willing servant—and He used this story to teach me what He desires for us, as well.

Elisha had some questions for this woman, and God is asking the same questions of us: *"What shall I do for you?"* and *"What do you have in the house?"* (2 Kings 4:2). To understand what this story means for us today, we're going to start with examining this woman's situation and what it symbolizes, because this story has some rich meaning. Then, we will spend some time on these questions Elisha asked, because God is asking His people the same revealing questions.

He wants to lead you to powerful answers that will unlock something great, not only for you, but for the world.

"But He's all-knowing," you might be thinking. "Why ask us questions?" Yes, He already knows the answer, but these questions will reveal things to us about ourselves He needs us to see. By letting God lay bare our hearts, He can lead us to a vital understanding of all the extras we've used to fill our lives—and His church. The precious woman in this story saw a great miracle come when she provided God what He needed to produce a miracle, and I believe the same thing can happen in our lives today if we do as she did: admit our emptiness so that we can be filled.

Built on Credit

Back when this story happened, a woman without a husband had few options. Women were not emancipated and actualized; they couldn't just go get a job. She'd be relying on her husband, and with him gone, her sons to come of age. If the creditors took her sons, she would be left literally with nothing—no prospects, no hope, no future—and her sons would be sold into a future of slavery.

Now, understand that the Old Testament is useful to us as a "type and shadow" (a foretelling of future things), and much of it is highly symbolic. As God showed me this passage, He revealed that the husband in this story represents the past, and the sons represent the future. God began to show me that the forerunners of the modern church and their actions have caused the present and future to be in slavery. The church fathers of yesterday created a deficit that the postmodern church is now accountable to pay, and the legacy they have left has no opportunity for a future, just like the sons, because it was based on traditions rather than the presence of God.

I'm not trying to disparage the great men and women of God who have gone before, since God has used some amazing people. Yet He

showed me that many of yesterday's actions were not built on *Him* but instead became about creating our own institutions. This has left us filled with many traditions and programs . . . but bereft of His *power.*

It's as though we've built all these things within the church on credit—a hollow, empty shell without the Spirit of God empowering it. We've operated on traditions and inertia; we do Church the way we do because it's how it's been done, or we seek to be relevant by catering to our culture. But now, today, we find that the bill is due, and the creditor is coming. And despite all the appearances—the buildings, the programs, the events—we have nothing of actual value because we have built on institutions of man rather than moves of God.

In some churches, it's become popular to try to revive old practices in hopes that the ways of the past would somehow create a revival in the present. They fail to realize that life isn't in the old practice; it's in God. If He isn't present in a thing, no matter how good it was in the past, it is the *old.* And God is interested in doing something *new.* If we try to get full with practices of the past rather than the promises of God, we're attempting to get full of something empty of Him. We cannot simply expect to live the way those before us did—we must continuously pursue God for what is *next.*

Know Him for Yourself

I recently had a conversation with my children. My daughter is the oldest, so I was mostly talking to her at the time, but I think it's the perfect illustration. I told them, "You can't find your way into the presence of God on the coattails of your father forever. My pressing in will not create your Presence. It may be while you're under my cover, but eventually, you'll grow up and need to press into God for yourself. You can't live off what God wanted for me—you'll need to get to know Him for yourselves."

The church leaders, like the father in our story of the widow and her sons, had created wealth, but now, just like him, they are gone, and you and I are here. At some point in the past, leaders were discipling believers; fathers and sons were creating generational wealth. But somewhere along the line, it became habitual, and gradually, we stopped developing creative new leaders, spiritual fathers stopped raising sons, and spiritual mothers ceased training daughters who could connect with God for themselves. We cannot rely on their relationship with God back in the day. Just like my kids, we all will someday need to get to know Him for ourselves. That day, my friend, is now.

I don't think I'm alone in having questions about the future of our nation, the church, and our lives and families. The last few years have shaken many people's trust in our institutions and traditions. From pandemics to politics, disasters to inflation, we've dealt with events that make us question whether the future holds promise or dread. The mere fact that we have such questions tells me that we have not had the vibrant relationship with God that is to be our rock and our hope in troubled times. It tells me that many things around us have been built on credit, on a promissory note, without real collateral.

We've lived on inertia, moving forward because that's what we do, but the foundation isn't the solid rock; it's on man's ways. Now, the bill is due, and the creditor is at the door with shackles in his hands, and our hollow human constructions are proving they cannot support our hope for the future. Unless we want our children to be bound as slaves to addiction, pain, sin, and deconstruction, we need to make immediate and lasting changes. Trying to fill up on man's creations, instead of relying on God to build the house, has gotten us into trouble.

Some say the church is no longer relevant, but that's untrue. We're just as relevant as we've ever been because the Spirit of God is relevant. But we must decide if we want to carry that relevance to the world or continue to build our own institutions, full of things that are not of eternal worth.

Church, *as we've done it* in America, *is* in trouble. Fewer people claim to be believers now than ever—some studies say it's down from 90 percent fifty years ago to just 64 percent as I write this.[1] Numbers in most churches never fully rebounded after the COVID pandemic, and church membership is down across the board. Many are disillusioned, but young people show a particularly stark decline in faith. And yet, I believe that young people will be a significant part of a great move of God that is coming because they have grown up in a culture of inconsistencies and facades and are searching for truth and authenticity.

THE WORLD'S CONDITION IS DIRECTLY RELATED TO THE CHURCH

This shows why there's so much bondage, depression, and brokenness present in the world. The world's condition is directly related to the church; *we* determine the state of the world. The enemy wants to tell you a lie that the church isn't relevant, but that's never been true. Our current state is because we're bankrupt and trying to live on what others built before rather than what the Spirit is doing now.

For too long, the same bug that bit the world has also bitten the church. We've been obsessed with our fulfillment, success, and opportunity. Along the way, we left God out in exchange for tradition or cultural relevance. We thought we could arrive at our destiny—going

---

[1] https://www.cnn.com/2023/04/08/us/christianity-decline-easter-blake-cec/index.html#:~:text=That%20same%20survey%20said%20the,slightly%20below%20pre%2D-pandemic%20levels

into all the world to preach the gospel of Jesus Christ—through programs, but we left behind dependence on our Creator. We replaced His life and power with institutions and clichés.

It's no wonder so many people are without hope! They've put their hope in all the wrong things. You may know that if you put your hope in politics, the politicians will disappoint you. The system will let you down, and it's incapable of changing what really matters. If you put your hope in the organized church, running on the power of the past without fresh life, you will be crushed as you watch people leave it.

We've tried to live on what I call pseudo-hope. We say, "I hope I'll get there." We think that if we keep trying long enough, with good enough intentions, somehow it might be okay. Yet this isn't biblical hope; it's wishful thinking. Real hope is in God, and we will never be disappointed when it is rooted solely in Him.

The church is the only hope for the world. I don't mean our institutions or buildings; I mean the Body of Christ—you and me. When we're in love with Jesus, serving Him, listening to Him, and moving as He says to move, we become part of something solid enough for a lost world to find hope in. When we stop making it about us and begin saying only what we hear our Father say, we open the door to God moving powerfully. People will see that, and then they will find hope in God alone.

We don't find our destiny without the divine. We can't see where we're going without the guidance of the One who has set us on our journey; so we will only find our destiny when we tune in to God's GPS, which guides us to our destination. He created our starting place and has a purpose for our lives as we navigate to His goal.

Our hope isn't in church traditions; it's in the person of Jesus Christ. God desires to create an awakening so that we don't find our future and the future of our children bound by the debt created by living off credit. Instead of a church built on the old, God has something fresh and new. Now that's something to be hopeful about!

What Do You Have in Your House?

Let's go back to our story. I mentioned the revealing questions the prophet asked, and God is asking us, so let's look at those now. Elisha asked the widow, "What shall I do for you?" Oddly, he didn't wait for her answer; he began another track that revealed the state of her life. In the same way, God asks that of His people—what would we have Him do for us—and He follows it up with a revealing question that lays bare the state of our hearts.

Elisha immediately followed his first question by asking, "Tell me, what do you have in the house?" This is a question for her but also for us as individuals and as members of the church.

God is a gentleman, and He will not force Himself on us. He stands at the doorway, asking us what we want Him to do for us and revealing our hearts. Remember, He's not asking because He lacks knowledge; He's asking because *we* lack it. Before He starts doing anything, He wants *us* to understand what we have inside us. God is prepared to move, but first, we must evaluate ourselves.

The first question He asks is what we want Him to do for us. The fact is, we don't even really know what God is *capable* of doing. God tells us, *"For My thoughts are not your thoughts, nor are your ways My ways," says the Lord. "For as the heavens are higher than the Earth, so are My ways higher than your ways, and My thoughts than your thoughts"* (Isaiah 55:8-9). We can't even fathom what He can do if the Holy Spirit doesn't reveal it. But God already knows what He wants to do on the Earth; He wants us to get on board.

To help us get behind His intentions for the Earth, He has to show us something—that all the *stuff* with which we've filled our lives is worthless—so He asks us, *"What do you have in the house?"* (2 Kings

4:2). And this woman was amazing because she was brutally honest as she replied, *"Your maidservant has nothing in the house but a jar of oil"* (2 Kings 4:2).

Now, do you think she really had bare walls, no furniture, and nothing on the shelves—a truly empty house? She understood that Elisha was asking what she had of *value*, and this is why it's so important to understand the difference between all the stuff with which we fill our lives and that which has real, lasting value. She may have had all kinds of items in her house, but the creditor was about to claim them. So she was honest, revealing that nothing in her home had worth—well, *almost* nothing, but we'll get to that in a moment.

Will we be as honest as she was? "God," we may answer, "I do all these activities. I'm involved in these things at church. I read these books, do these good deeds, know these people." You may have a lot of stuff in your life, but it's hollow if it's not focused on Him.

The exact same thing is true of the church. What do we have in God's house? The postmodern church has stuff—it's just not stuff of value. We've got chairs and lights, sound systems and a band, maybe even smoke machines and lasers, but these things are just baggage without the power of God behind them.

Fatherless

The woman answered Elisha, *"Your maidservant has nothing,"* which helped explain the situation she was in. It explains the condition of the church, as well. Fascinatingly, the Hebrew word used here for "nothing" could also be translated as "fatherless." The widow was in her situation because the father had left the picture.

Remember what I said at the beginning—that the father represents the past. In the church, we have had "fathers," great men and women of God who laid a foundation of the powerful ministry God did through them. But we now find ourselves filled with stuff of no value because

we've tried to operate on the outpouring from the past, instead of a current relationship with *the Father*. Only when we have the Father do we have something of value (Him) to pay the debt against us (sin). It's a debt we cannot pay with good works and outreach programs. Without the value brought by the Father, all the stuff in our churches is revealed as empty by the state of the world we are to influence. If the world's falling apart (which it is), it shows that the church has nothing to offer—we've become Fatherless. And what is true of the church can be true in our lives, too, for so many believers are not Father-focused.

If this has sounded like a strong indictment of today's church, it is— but it's necessary to see what the widow admitted: We have nothing of value without the Father. But God did not leave her destitute and hopeless, and He doesn't leave us that way either.

God has something great in store for us, His people, and He, not the creditor, is standing at our door *right now* and asking revealing questions so we will come to the realizations that set us free. Only when we admit that we have nothing of value without Him, can we become empty of all the other stuff we've tried to use to get full.

CHAPTER 3:

GOD WANTS EMPTY VESSELS

IN THE PREVIOUS CHAPTER, we saw that while many churches and individuals have filled our lives with things that don't have value, some still have a little left over from when the Spirit of God was moving powerfully. In our story of the widow and Elisha, at first, she said she had nothing. But then she amends her statement and adds, *"Your maidservant has nothing in the house but a jar of oil"* (2 Kings 4:2). She reveals she had something so small that she almost overlooked it: She had a little jar of old oil. Let's dive back into this example from Scripture and see what God does.

In the Bible, oil represents the Holy Spirit. Looking around the church, I still see evidence that some jars still have a little oil. Many moves of God and churches start so powerfully, but they seem to run their course over time. Where once the oil of the Spirit flowed freely, eventually we seem to lose sight of how we had been filled initially. That means all too often, the Body of Christ is trying to break the

curses over families, see people set free of bondage, and bring peace to people and nations, while operating on just a little leftover oil.

You need fresh oil in your life, just as much as the church does.

Are you worried? Troubled? Sick? Depressed? You need a new supply of the Holy Spirit! I'm sure you want to see loved ones set free, coworkers come to Jesus, troubled kids find peace, and the sick healed. You want the Word to come alive as you read it, the songs you sing to be worship, and peace to overwhelm your troubles.

So, how long will you try to function on old oil?

In the Old Testament, they used oil for many things, from cooking to medicine. No doubt, this woman once had a much larger supply of oil when the father was in the house. Maybe it started in a bigger vessel, but as it got lower and lower, perhaps she downsized her expectations and moved it to a little jar.

But God doesn't want to work with little jars—He's got something bigger in mind. He's tired of us putting constraints around our expectations of Him, downsizing Him by what we've seen lately. Our perspective of Him has become so small!

God doesn't want jars. He wants *vessels*!

And here's the key: God only wants vessels without *anything* in them. He doesn't want full vessels or ones that are half full. He needs them (us) to be empty because He's about to fill us up!

In our story, Elisha tells the widow to borrow empty vessels from her neighbors, as many as she can find. It doesn't matter what color they are, what shape they are, or even if they have cracks in them. They just need to be *empty*.

It's time to let go of all the stuff we've filled up and pour it out so that our vessels can be empty. God doesn't want our sacrifices, programs, activities, or best intentions. He doesn't want anything we've worked up because He doesn't want us to try to take credit for the pour.

When We Bring Him Empty, God Begins to Move

Nothing happened until the house was full of empty vessels, and only then did the Spirit of God begin to move. So, as individuals and as a church, we need to shut the door and leave behind all the ideas and agendas of the world so that God may pour His Spirit into us.

When we come empty into His presence, without pretense or filler, it inspires something to pour out from Heaven that will not quit pouring until all the available room is full. That's why we must be empty; we can't be contaminated by something else in the vessel. God will not share space, but when we bring Him empty, God begins to move.

This woman gathered all the vessels from her neighbors she was able, and once she had as many as she could find, she and her sons went into their house and shut the door. She took that little jar of old oil in her hand, and as she began to pour into empty vessels, God began to do the miraculous.

She poured, God multiplied, and the first big empty vessel began to fill up. The little jar couldn't hold much, yet out of it poured more and more oil. A miracle happened as her tiny jar filled first one vessel, then another. As each filled up, they set it aside and moved to the next in line. Empty vessel after empty vessel filled up with clear, fresh oil as she worked her way through every one of them in the house. Until, finally, when she filled the last vessel, the flow stopped.

God had divinely multiplied the oil she had, and that little bit of oil didn't stop pouring until she had filled up every vessel in her entire house. Can you imagine her excitement as she flung open her door and ran back to Elisha to tell him what God had done?

God had filled up all those empty vessels, but there was one more part to her miracle. When she told Elisha what the Lord had done, he told her to sell the oil to pay her debt—and that there would be oil left from which she and her sons could live. That must've been a lot of oil she'd poured into many empty vessels!

God had *filled* her house with *value*. While once it had lacked anything of worth, it now contained greatness—the oil of the Lord.

Go Into All the World

Don't you crave being filled with the presence of the Lord? To have your vessel filled up with Him, instead of all the hollow things of this world that can never satisfy? My dream for you and God's church is that we all are filled to the brim. But what comes next?

God had filled the house, but now the widow had something she must do—empty it again. She'd brought empty vessels in, God filled them, and now she would carry them out into the world. Elisha told her to sell them so she and her sons could live.

Interestingly, the word used in the text for "sell" could also be translated as "surrender" or "give up." I love this because that's exactly what God wants to do with us: fill us up . . . so we can give it away.

God doesn't fill us with His presence so we can hoard it and have a house filled with oil. We are to bring that oil out into the world and give it away so that lost and hurting people all over can see the power and value of vessels filled with His presence!

We're comfortable with the idea of God filling His house with His presence, but that is not the end of the story. Remember, He calls those who know their emptiness, as the master did for the wedding feast where they went into the highways and hedges. As God fills us, His vessels, we must then open the closed doors we've been behind as we shut out the world and now go out into it empowered by the presence of God.

It's important to consider that the oil isn't ours; it's His. We don't create it, and we don't get to hoard it away. When Jesus multiplied the loaves and fish (see Matthew 15:33-38), He didn't do so just so the disciples could eat. He had them take the pieces and give them away.

As we share the oil God gives us, we show God we are those He can pour through. It's not just meant for us—our personal lives and churches. It's intended for the world! He wants to send us out of His house and use us to fill the Earth with His presence.

How can we fulfill God's Great Commission to go into all the world and make disciples? Only through the power and presence of His Holy Spirit. That's why the Spirit had to fall on the believers at Pentecost— He needed to empower them to be His vessels and spread the Good News throughout the Earth.

The church has not become irrelevant; we've been cluttered and full of the wrong things, and the state of the world shows this clearly. So, what could God do through us if we were instead filled with His presence and then brought that out into the world? We would experience a great move of God!

No one knows the day or hour of Christ's return, but we are closer now than ever. Something in me feels like we may have only one more great outpouring of His presence before the end, and the Lord knows that our world desperately needs it! This world is hungry and broken, and they're looking for something to satisfy them. They've tried the rest and seen how worthless it all is. They see how empty they are, and that will make them perfect vessels to be brought in and filled with the power of God's presence.

But how will they hear unless we share the Good News with them?

God is calling us empty vessels filled with His power to go into all the world. Not just where we're comfortable or where it's convenient. He's calling us to where there's lack and deficit. The oil isn't needed in a house full of it; it's needed *out there*, where their jars and vessels are bone dry. He needs us to carry the oil where it doesn't look good, feel good, or smell good, where there are people who we don't like or who make us uncomfortable, where they are hurting, broken, angry, and bitter. These people may take a swing at us because they're striking

out at anything that's around them. But these people are the very ones God wants to redeem and heal.

Emptiness Creates Overflow

Interestingly, the widow's miracle didn't stop when the vessels were filled. She didn't just live in a house of full containers because having full vessels did not bring her or her sons' life. Carrying the oil out of the house and *distributing* it brought life.

You might be thinking, "This doesn't make any sense. God wants me empty so He can fill me up . . . so He can empty me again?"

Yes. God moves when we're empty! He can fill us when there's nothing in our vessel. The world desperately needs what we have when God fills us up. They're dry and broken, and they need empty vessels (us) who can get filled up (with His power and presence) in His house (churches) so He can pour out His Spirit to those who are dying and headed to destruction all around us.

God wants to fill us up but doesn't want us to be filled up with no outlet. Do you know what they call it when a body of water gets filled up but has no outlet? A dead sea. You go brackish and dead if you're not, in turn, pouring out after you've been filled. Pouring out is the key to being emptied again, ready to be filled once more—which is how we stay full of *fresh* oil, instead of it getting old by just sitting around. In this way, God ministers to the lost and hurting *through us*. When we carry the oil outside the house of God into the dry places, not only will we live, but so will the generations after us and those around us who are perishing.

God is not worried about the state of the world in which we live; He knows He needs those who will bring their empty vessels to Him, so that we may be filled up, and then share Him with the world. That is the path to the move of God we so desperately need!

Emptiness creates overflow. This is the opposite of what the world says—that we must fill our lives up. Instead, it's our emptiness, in the hands of God, that eliminates deficit.

EMPTINESS CREATES OVERFLOW.

If we want to see changes in our culture, country, city, friends, and families, we aren't to look to Washington. God doesn't depend on politicians for the changes we need. He's looking for a house, and a person who will bring Him empty vessels—and the overflow will find its way to Washington and beyond.

We won't experience the overflow if we settle for being filled with worthless things. We won't experience it if we settle for a little jar of old oil. Fresh oil is only provoked by our emptiness, our hunger for God.

God is at the door, ready to pour. He is prepared to move! Yet He needs you, He needs me, and He needs a church that will set aside all the extra things we've filled up with so He can fill our empty vessels.

When Jesus arrived on the scene, He said, "Repent!" Repenting means turning away, and this is what God is calling us to do now, as well. We've tried to do God's work with a little bit of old oil—a little bit of God and a large amount of us—but it's time to repent, because this won't work. It's not enough to meet the deep needs of the broken world around us. We can't rely on the leftovers of what God did in the past because He has a new thing He wants to do in the Earth.

God is standing at your door, knocking. He wants to ask you what you have in your house. Are you willing to evaluate what's in your house? If you're honest enough to say, "Nothing," God is ready to pour Himself out.

I don't know what your next season holds, but we stand at the door of great opportunity to see the manifestation and move of God on the

Earth. Some may not be willing to evaluate what's in their house—they may be okay with just the little bit of leftover oil they have left, or a home filled with stuff bought on credit. But if you feel like God is calling you to something deeper, that will be genuinely fulfilling at the deepest level of your spirit, admit your emptiness to Him. Repent of trying to fill up on all the extras of this world and let Him instead fill you with the might and power of His presence!

God doesn't need you to have the answers. He doesn't need your plans or your money. He needs you to be empty—ready for Him to fill.

He's standing at your door, knocking. How will you answer?

CHAPTER 4:
MY BROKENNESS

IN THE PREVIOUS CHAPTERS, I have tried to describe what God showed me for His people and His church—a powerful image of being emptied of all the extras of life so that we can be filled with the only One who really matters. The problem is that God can show us principles from His Word and give us life-giving instructions, but they will not become real until we see them in operation in our own lives.

I shared with you God's message to His people to enter empty, but I have a personal story of being emptied, broken at the feet of Jesus, and unable to do anything but rely on Him. To me, this isn't just a message; it's something I've been living.

The term brokenness sometimes seems confusing in the church because we use it for different things. Sometimes, people use it as a term for having been through loss or feeling destroyed. Many people may feel abused, crushed, or even assaulted by life and by events outside of their control that leave them traumatized.

But when I say broken, I am speaking of something different. David writes, *"For You do not desire sacrifice, or else I would give it; You do not delight in burnt offering. The sacrifices of God are a broken spirit, a broken and a contrite heart—these, O God, You will not despise"* (Psalm 51:16-17). David is not speaking of a crushed, destroyed spirit; he's speaking of a tender, humbled heart laid at the feet of God. Biblical brokenness is a realization that there's nothing of value in my life without the presence of the Lord, a hunger for Him, and a realization that we have no capacity for anything good or to even live life without Him.

This life throws many things at us, and sometimes, our damage and trauma are what leads us to this brokenness in spirit. It's not that God is thrusting bad things upon us, but sometimes we get to a place of a broken spirit and contrite heart because of the trials of life.

Consider this: Pursuing this life leads to being filled with things that will ultimately destroy us. The pleasures of this world, our modern culture, and even our worldly success can all seem like things that will fulfill and satisfy, but when we are filling up with them instead of God, we are actively chasing our pain. How often have you put your hope in a job, someone's reaction, possessions, wealth, or some other temporary thing, only to learn the hard way that putting your hope in these inevitably leads to disappointment?

We can be so blinded by the pursuit of the things of this world that it's only when it has all crumbled to ash that our eyes are opened. We can be consumed with wanting what we want and we won't stop until we get it. And then we do, and all those things we thought would fulfill instead leave us burned out and crushed . . . and yet ready to be spiritually broken and empty.

I'm reminded of the story of the prodigal son, who got everything he wanted—the money, the travel, the friends, the parties—and only realized what he really had when it all came crashing down. Hungrily eyeing the food he was giving the pigs that he'd been reduced to tending, we read, ***"But when he came to himself,*** *he said, 'How many* *of my father's hired servants have bread enough and to spare, and I perish with hunger!"* (Luke 15:17, emphasis mine)

This is brokenness—a humbled, repentant heart.

We wonder why God "permits" this stuff to happen to us, but God has no choice because we control the permission of our lives. If that rubs some of you wrong, consider this—God has given us free will, and He is not going to override the authority He has given us. He's not going to intervene until we permit Him to do so by repenting and inviting Him in. That is why we may be crushed and assaulted by life, which leads to brokenness, and in that place of humility, we empty ourselves . . . so we may be filled. The prodigal returned home, and his father filled him once more: a ring for his finger, a robe on his back, and sandals on his feet. He was once again restored to the operational status of his sonship after he came to his senses and a broken spirit. When he recognized his emptiness, he could then be filled.

I tell you all of this, so you'll have a context for my journey of brokenness.

A Spiritual Father

I come from a broken family; much of what was going on around me was dysfunctional. We faced constant battles, court systems, addictions to "street pharm" and prescription meds, alcohol abuse, rebellion, demonic oppression, and even religion. Because of it, I have siblings who have been tormented with addiction and loss, including my sister Kelsey. Thankfully, Kelsey, along with her husband, Chris, experienced a life-changing encounter with the Father that restored their lives and their family. Now, they lead the restoration ministry at our church.

My father raised me as a single parent. He provided for me, disciplined me, and kept me inside the church, but my childhood was a

place of severe deficit, rejection and pain, void of self-esteem, and hunger for affirmation and identity.

I turned to so many things to fill myself up, to cover over the void left by my dysfunctional family. My drug of choice was women, and I tried to find love, affirmation, and feeling wanted by chasing them, and football, as well. They weren't all bad, but I tried to make stuff like sports fill a void that these things were never intended to fill. It was only later in life that God got ahold of me and put a call on my life.

After years of not knowing how my call fit in the church, I gained a spiritual father in Bishop Tony Miller. I first encountered Bishop early in my surrender, not long before I really got involved in regular ministry—probably sometime around 2005. He was a distant voice for many years, but I really did not engage deeply until the mid-2010s. We were both at a mutual friend's house late one night after a service and were just drawn together. From there, he invited me out to Oklahoma City. For many years, we lived in the same city, but it wasn't until we were a thousand miles apart that God bound our lives together.

I mentioned Bishop in the first chapter when I shared that God gave him and me the same image of a great feast. This was a precious interaction with Bishop because God began giving me this message on how to enter empty at the end of 2020, and I began to preach it as 2021 dawned.

Bishop Miller died on January 19, 2021, during the *Enter Empty* series I was preaching.

I had flown down to meet with him in Denton, Texas, and the night before we were to meet, I got a call that froze me in my place. I was in my hotel room and in utter shock: Bishop had died. I've had other people pass away in my life—grandparents and others who were close to me—but I must say, this was one of the most traumatic losses of my life because of the significance Bishop Miller had been to me. He had seen something in me and was a spiritual father I desperately needed.

I had run from the call of God on my life for over six years and had never been mentored, but Bishop Miller had seen the call God placed on my life and nurtured it. I don't think I totally understood how much I craved that until he was gone.

I must confess, I felt very selfish as I sat frozen at the news of his death. I was brokenhearted, but I kept wondering, "What am I going to do now, God?" Without him, I had nobody to help me. I didn't know what to do. I felt gutted. He'd been the most influential man in my life over the last several years, maybe in my lifetime, but in the last year or so we had gotten close. It was entering a deep significance . . . and now he was gone. Bishop had opened doors for me I never expected to walk through, and our spiritual DNA had been so similar. He was an inspiration to me. I had just spent a week with him and his family at his home before Christmas and now, a month later, he was gone. How?

Fear overtook me. If this could happen to a sixty-three-year-old man of God operating in his spiritual prime, I wondered what hope I had. I was actually afraid to get back on an airplane and fly home! I think I managed to get on the plane because of a combination of the facts that I didn't have a choice, I had to face my fears, and I really wanted to see my wife and children.

I also got a couple of phone calls and prophetic words while I was in that hotel room. A friend of mine, who is in ministry, called. All I remember him saying was something about a "passing of the baton." I had literally had the thought of the baton on my mind for about a month and didn't know why. Another man I met through Bishop Tony, who has now become such a spiritual mentor, confidant, and even father-like figure in my life, is Apostle Les Bowling. He also called me late that night, and we talked things through a little bit; he's such an encouraging voice.

I could not see at the time that God had something to show me: I needed no man to open doors for me that He would open, and God

was passing on to me a spiritual mantle. Bishop Miller carried an incredible anointing, but God began to reveal that He had something for me as well, something inspired by this great man like Elisha was by Elijah. God opened a door for me, a spiritual invitation into a new level with Him, but I had no idea what I would be going through as God removed all the props I thought I needed so that I could enter this new place empty.

No More Crutches

It felt like the loss of Bishop Miller began a dark, unpleasant road as, one piece at a time, God started to empty me of everything on which I'd leaned. Soon, division sprang up within my church, and we had trouble with several staff members. We had a healthy church, so it was a massive surprise to have such tension and division. I missed being able to call Bishop Miller for support.

The weight and pressure of Bishop's loss, the problems in the church, and other things began to weigh on me. I can remember being in a staff meeting when I said that while I was spiritually okay, I had to admit to them that I was mentally and emotionally exhausted. Honestly, I didn't know how I was functioning.

But it was more than just stress. In hindsight, something wasn't right inside me, physically. I didn't know it yet, but I was about to experience a trial in my health—and was probably feeling the first effects of it—that would challenge me in every possible way.

By November of 2021, I had reached a new place with God because I honestly had no alternative but to lean on Him. Sitting on my porch and looking at the trees, I remember crying out to God. "I've got nothing left," I told Him, "I'm spent!"

As I cried out to the Lord, a new prayer began welling up in me: "God, I don't want all your exploits and all these things. I don't care about the power and demonstration. I just want to know Your heart."

I felt like God answered, "Okay, but know that you had better be careful what you're asking because I am going to carry you into a place that you could not have gone when healthy.

"There are places in your life that have looked healthy—you've been able to move past some things mentally and emotionally—so you can function, but nevertheless, there is some deep sepsis. If I don't uncover these places and touch them, they will become places that the enemy will riddle with insecurities, especially at the levels to which I'm calling you.

SONS BECOME FATHERS.

"I'm about to peel back layers of your life like an onion, removing the layers of skin from your life that have covered over what's still dead so I can touch those places. I'm going to teach you what it is to be a son because, while I've called you to be a spiritual father, you must first learn how to be a son. After all, sons become fathers."

That was a sobering word, but nothing seemed to happen for weeks. Then, in February of 2022, something happened suddenly: I had to go to the hospital with my heart hammering out of my chest. God had begun His deep work, and now the peel of my health was being laid back.

Job Situation

In the book of Job, we read of a godly man afflicted by great adversity. In the same breath, it was 100 percent God working, but it was also the enemy's attack. That was my experience for the next few years of my life.

Symptoms began to wrack my body, and I went to doctors and hospitals, everywhere I could, to learn what was wrong, only to be told it was allergies or some other misdiagnosis. They did X-rays and MRIs, but nothing was wrong with my head. They did EKGs, but nothing was wrong with my heart. But pressure, dizziness, ringing in my ears, light-headedness, confusion, and difficulty focusing my vision dominated my days, sapped my strength, and made me wonder if I was going crazy. My nervous system was going haywire, and I dealt with symptoms in every system of my body. Anxiety, panic, and depression followed, but no one could tell me what was wrong. I felt like I was dying! I couldn't think, felt constantly lethargic, and didn't have the energy to have a conversation with people or sometimes even be in my own skin.

After a long time, a thought came to my spirit: Test the air. I had testing done, and it returned positive for mold at our home—and in our old church offices. We ended up having our house's ductwork replaced, along with the air conditioning and heater, but I had been getting it in two places, both at home and at work. A flood in 2020 affected the house, but the offices were just old, so while my immediate family had experienced some of the same symptoms I did, I was in it daily at home and at work for some time. My body had gone toxic. Between mold and EMF radiation, the toxicity had caused everything in my body to enter into chronic inflammation.

It was debilitating. I couldn't travel and had a hard time functioning at all. I had to lean so heavily on the Lord just to operate! It got so bad over such a long period of time that I forgot what normal felt like. I'd always been able to rely on my body, play sports, and be physically active. Now, God had removed the crutch of my health. I felt like Job.

That was the physical side, but there was a spiritual one as well. The worst part was that God had been speaking to me clearly, telling me about the cleansing work He would be doing and revealing other parts of His will to me. And then, suddenly, He went silent. It was so odd because I felt like I could sense Him in my spirit, which is how

I could still preach, but it felt like He didn't *speak* to me . . . for over two years.

Broken Prayers

Tim Keller shared a message on Job that really ministered to me. He pointed out that most of Job's prayers were angry and fussing, complaining to God. They weren't prayers we'd think of as "good" prayers. So how could God eventually say that Job was His man and that his friends should have *Job* pray for *them*?

Despite all Job went through, he never left God. He laid all his cares at God's feet, even when nothing seemed to change for the better—even when it went from bad to *worse*. Despite it all, Job clung to God, His word, and His promises, and that's where he stayed. Even when he was complaining and crying out to God, Job was hanging onto Him—*and nothing else.*

Job was emptied of everything else in his life. He had no pretensions or crutches, nothing he could lean on but God Himself.

I know that place because that's where I have been. I pursued God in the years since I got sick more than I ever have in my entire life. When I shared the message that God wants us to enter empty with my congregation, I had no idea I would be living it in such a tangible way.

God was teaching me His love for a son who could do nothing to earn that love. It's almost like He had to teach me His love by what feels like being unlovable. A mantle of anointing was shifting, but it would not come without a price. Everything I went through has resulted in a great hunger for God's presence, and I will not be satisfied with anything else. It's not enough anymore to fill my life with *stuff*; I desire only to be filled with His presence.

And that is my prayer for you as well—that you hunger to host God's presence.

Be, Not Do

It's tempting to think that connecting with God is an effort of our will or the result of diligently pursuing faith disciplines. Now, I'm never going to say we shouldn't pray or read our Bibles, but God showed me a very different side of abiding with Him during the course of my sickness. All those things are good, but the real key God was showing me was that I needed to spend time at the feet of Jesus.

One of the people who best showed this was Mary, who was the sister of Martha and Lazarus. When we first meet Mary and Martha, we read that Martha was distracted by serving Jesus' dinner, while Mary just sat at His feet and listened to the word. Martha complained to Jesus that her sister wasn't helping, to which Jesus replied, *"Martha, Martha, you are worried and troubled about many things. But one thing is needed, and Mary has chosen that good part, which will not be taken away from her"* (Luke 10:41-42).

HE HUNGERS FOR US TO SIT AT HIS FEET MORE.

Martha wasn't doing *bad* things, but Mary chose to sit at Jesus' feet. That's where I was because I could do little else! There are practical things we use to fill up our time with God—our agenda of prayers, meditation, and reading the Word. But He hungers for us to sit at His feet more.

I learned this firsthand. I used to wonder how I should pray—how should I sit, do I bow my head, should I close my eyes? But I remember one day, when I had just been pushing it for some time and was exhausted. When I spend time with God in the morning, I often go into my office and lie on my face on the floor. But I was so tired that when I laid on my face to pray and meditate . . . I fell asleep!

When I woke up, I felt so horrible. I had screwed up, falling asleep on the Lord. But I felt like God asked me why I thought I needed some regimented practice to spend time with Him. I felt Him asking, "Don't you know that you can lay down and rest in My presence?" At that moment, a burden lifted off my life. I had peace that I could lay down and rest in God's presence. Now, I'm not going to take a nap every time I intend to meet with God, but He showed me it wasn't what I was *doing* that mattered—it's Who I was *with*.

"Your heart was still after me," I felt like God said, "and everything else was pushed aside for that moment with me. Lay down, my son, and rest." This echoed what Jesus had said: *"Are you tired? Worn out? Burned out on religion? Come to me. Get away with me, and you'll recover your life. I'll show you how to take a real rest. Walk with me and work with me—watch how I do it. Learn the unforced rhythms of grace. I won't lay anything heavy or ill-fitting on you. Keep company with me, and you'll learn to live freely and lightly"* (Matthew 11:28-30 MSG).

Ask this of yourself: Are you tired and worn out? Do you feel like the burden you're under is easy and light? Do you feel like the requirements put on your life, church, and relationship with God fit this description of how Jesus does it? Religious tradition has filled us with many demands, but I pray that God lifts the yoke of these requirements and exchanges them for the gentle, light yoke of Christ, in whom we find our rest.

We have filled our lives with so many things that weigh us down, but that is not God's will for us. God wants to simplify our walk with Him. We've been burdened by many calls: Do this or do that to be good believers. It's burned so many out on "religion." But we are not to be guided by many voices; we're to be led by one voice—that of the Good Shepherd. And we were never called to be *religious* but to be *relational*. Our *doing* comes out of our *being*. We respond to God in active obedience because of our love and adoration for Him.

As a result of all my experiences, my pursuit of God has changed. I now understand that God is not after our mental assent or awareness. We're not after an informational awareness *about* God; we should crave to be filled with the presence of the Lord like people who are dying of thirst and longing to drink deeply of living water. I pray that through this book you meet with the living God, and begin to know Him and His love for you better, by emptying yourself of anything holding you back from drawing deeply on His incomparable presence.

To me, it's all about His presence and learning how to host more and more of Him in our lives. I want to practice presence and for us to be a presence-driven people. It isn't about our performance; it's about His presence.

Find Your Identity in Christ

Believers, as a group, have an identity crisis. What does it mean to be a son or daughter of God? Is it your behavior? Is it the things with which you fill up your day? Or is it the One we know intimately?

> BELIEVERS, AS A GROUP, HAVE AN IDENTITY CRISIS.

The Bible is a Father-Son story. We fit in as the adopted kids who find our identity in the firstborn, Jesus. We can only find our own identity when we find ourselves in Him.

For so many, faith seems enigmatic and ill-defined. They're confused. But Hebrews 11 teaches us that faith is the *substance* of things hoped for and the *evidence* of the things we cannot yet see. It's not mysterious—it's both substance and evidence. So, what is that substance and evidence? It's God! It's His presence, indwelling and transforming us from the inside out. Religion tries to shape you from the outside in, but God has begun a work in each of us that He is faithful to complete and will transform us into sons and daughters in the pattern of Jesus.

Jesus did not grasp at godliness; He just walked in His Father's footsteps. He said what the Father said and did what He did. But Jesus did it all full of the Spirit, and so it is with us—we are like our Father and His Son when we are full of His Holy Spirit.

So many believers are struggling with an identity issue because they've made it about their behavior. Still, few have understood the real problem: We are trying to fill ourselves up and find our identity with actions, not presence. But when we clear all the extra out of our vessels, that emptiness is the genesis of true identity in Christ. This is how we meet that hunger to know who we are, what we are to do, why our lives matter, and what our value is. None of those answers are found in the filler.

OUR PURPOSE IS SIMPLY THIS: TO BE VESSELS OF HIS PRESENCE.

Our purpose is simply this: to be vessels of His presence.

If you have read the self-help books, tried the faith disciplines, been spinning your wheels, or stuck in the same cycle I was in, it's time to drop all the baggage and embrace emptiness. I had empty forced on me; I could do nothing else while I was so sick but rely on God. We discover our true identity when we realize our emptiness because only then can God fill us up with Himself.

Every human on the face of the Earth can find his or her true purpose at the beginning of the Bible from God's own words: *"Let Us make man in Our image, according to Our likeness"* (Genesis 1:26). You were made in the image of God.

You were made to be filled with His presence!

All that's necessary for you to walk in this as Jesus did is to become an empty vessel, surrendered to God, at peace in His unforced rhythms of grace.

When you do this, you will encounter the Creator of the Universe. It won't matter how strong you are, how long you can pray, or what other resources you have. (I know because I was stripped of my resources.) We were created only to have one source, God, and He promises that as we draw near to Him, He will draw near to us. He inhabits the praises of His people, so if you want to be filled with the presence of God, I urge you to lay aside every other yoke in exchange for one thing—that which is better, the same thing Mary found while Martha was so busy with all the stuff that filled her life: resting at the feet of Jesus.

CHAPTER 5:
POUR IT OUT

IN THE FIRST CHAPTERS, we looked at how God is standing at the door of our hearts, asking what we have in our house. Through the story of a widow whom God blessed through the Prophet Elisha, we see that when she admitted her emptiness, God told her how to get full. As she brought vessels into the house and shut the door to distractions, her emptiness created overflow. This is God's MO—He confounds the wise with His ways, which are so much higher than our ways—and works the impossible to fill our emptiness with His presence.

Now, you also know why this is so important to me personally. For two years, I could lean on nothing but God. If He did not fill me up, I could not function at all. I had to enter empty to survive, but God wasn't done affecting my life individually. He wanted to teach me how my willingness to be broken and empty before Him would impact the lives of others.

In the story of the woman with her little jar of oil, we saw something else that's so important that I want to drill into it even more in this chapter. God's purpose didn't end with a house full of filled vessels; God then had her *distribute* what He had given her, and through that, He provided for her—and others. This woman's story is far from the only example of someone taking a step of faith, so I want to take you

to another story in Scripture. Let's spend a little more time on the idea that it isn't just about being filled up; it's also vital that we pour out.

Giving away that which we just received seems unnatural. You'd think that if you were once empty and God filled you up, you should do all you can to hold onto that fullness, right? Instead, God calls us to empty ourselves again, to pour out what He has given to us so He can fill us once more. This is truly a Kingdom mentality, and it has to do with the fact that we aren't called to be filled just for our benefit but to be a blessing to others.

As God showed this to me, He took me to a famous story from the life of Elisha's spiritual father, Elijah. Elijah is perhaps the most famous of the Old Testament prophets. The last man standing in a faceoff with hundreds of prophets of the false god, Baal, as well as a murderous queen and a corrupt king, Elijah was God's vessel for speaking to His people and performing some mighty miracles.

Elijah would see fire fall from Heaven and one day rose to eternity in a flaming chariot rather than dying. However, God brought me to a more foundational miracle at the beginning of the prophet's story that echoes the miracle we just read about in Chapter Two.

Before Elijah's greatest acts of obedience and God's miracles, God told him to pray. But this was no ordinary prayer, "God, bless so-and-so." God told him to pray for something very specific, and it's our introduction to this man of God: The Lord told him to pray it wouldn't rain. And it didn't.

God was proving a point to His wayward people and their rebellious rulers, but He provided for Elijah. And later, He provided *through* him and a different widow. I love that God points out how He cares for widows and orphans throughout Scripture, proving Himself faithful. As we're about to see, He didn't just take care of the "man of God," He looked after another destitute widow and her son as they faced death by starvation.

Sent Word

We pick up the story after Elijah's prayer had resulted in a closed heaven and drought. At first, God cared for Elijah in the wilderness, commanding wild animals to bring him food while he drank from a stream. Yet, even that stream dried up, and finally, when the water stopped entirely, God called Elijah to go into town, where his life would touch another.

> *Then the word of the Lord came to him, saying, 'Arise, go to Zarephath, which belongs to Sidon, and dwell there. See, I have commanded a widow there to provide for you.' So he arose and went to Zarephath. And when he came to the gate of the city, indeed a widow was there gathering sticks. And he called to her and said, 'Please bring me a little water in a cup, that I may drink.' And as she was going to get it, he called to her and said, 'Please bring me a morsel of bread in your hand.'*

> 1 Kings 17:8-11

Zarephath was a Palestinian territory and a stronghold of the false god Baal. A stronghold is like a castle, but spiritually, it represents things like authority. It's designed to prevent things from getting in. Zarephath had been taken captive by the spirit of the age (Baal), so Elijah wasn't going to a hometown crowd that would be friendly to him. In essence, God was sending him into the very stronghold of the enemy.

Have you prayed and told God you'd do anything for Him, go anywhere . . . except *there* (wherever *there* was for you)? When God sends us with a word, it's often to places we don't want to go—and that would've been Zarephath for Elijah. After we've entered empty and been filled with God's Spirit, we may think He'll send us to welcoming people who will eagerly soak up what He wants us to pour out. But often, God sends us where we'd rather not go—uncomfortable places where the people are less-than-welcoming or even hostile. It can be

confusing because surely, if it were God, it would be *easy*, right? Not so much!

God desires to bring down the enemy's strongholds, which requires vessels filled with His presence to go into their midst and represent Him there. It was a stronghold of Baal for Elijah, but it will be different for us. In our era, the world can look a lot like Hell. Look at the wars, the famine, and the hostility toward the gospel, which can be intimidating. Your Zarephath may be your workplace, a friend group, or extended family. But strongholds aren't just places; they can be ideas.

Today, people seem to worship just about anything—but little of it is God. In fact, the most prevalent and fastest-growing "religion" isn't Christianity or Islam or some Eastern religion; it's secular humanism, which makes *us* "gods." It's the worship of self. The strongholds of today are not of false gods like Baal; they're strongholds of worship of ourselves.

My friend, God did not fill up our vessels so that we can be full; He has filled us up so that we can, in turn, pour out the Spirit of God into the very strongholds of the enemy. It's different for all of us, but some things remain the same—God will often call you to go right into the enemy's camp so you can be an insider, ready and positioned for His coming move.

In Romans 8:17, we are called sons and daughters of God, co-heirs with Christ, who will rule and reign with Him. When a ruler and children co-rule, it's because their kingdom has taken new territory. Our King desires to set His children, us, over the former strongholds of the false gods of this age.

God is sending a word through those who will stand up and be a prophetic voice in the world, taking responsibility for the Great Commission by walking into the enemy's strongholds carrying His Spirit with us. We are to go into territories held by the devil with a sent word from Heaven.

Isaiah wrote about this sent word: *"For as the rain comes down, and the snow from heaven, and do not return there, but water the earth, and make it bring forth and bud, that it may give seed to the sower and bread to the eater, so shall My word be that goes forth from My mouth; it shall not return to Me void, but it shall accomplish what I please, and it shall prosper in the thing for which I sent it"* (Isaiah 55:10).

God has a sent word from Heaven for His people to carry, but the problem is we have few *sent* men and women. Many feel they're *called*, but it's not always by God. Maybe they were called by a grandmother or an evangelist in a revival, but they want to go somewhere comfortable with things that make them feel fulfilled. Few are willing to be sent *anywhere* God wills. He's looking for people who will go wherever He sends us and say whatever He wants us to say.

Remember, God works through men and women. He doesn't just *poof*, plop His word out of Heaven, and we all see clouds of glory fall like glitter. Yes, He sends His word, but He sends it through *us*. Great moves of God have obedient vessels carrying His word to accomplish what He pleases. God is sending a word to us today, and the word of God is powerful to create, move, provoke, and bring life, but He needs sent men and women who will pour it out, even in uncomfortable places.

God's word is ready to accomplish great things, but He needs us to pour it out. Will you?

A Chosen Vessel

I find it interesting that God sent Elijah to a stronghold of Baal to dwell—and to a *widow* who would provide for him. This is backward because, as we saw with our last widow, she would've been a destitute woman, and there was a famine in the land! God was sending Elijah to an enemy stronghold and to someone weak, hurt, broken, and confused. On the surface, she had nothing to provide for him, but God had other plans.

The word "provide" used in the verse means "to contain" or "to receive." God was telling Elijah that He was sending the prophet to someone, a vessel, which would contain his presence—someone with space enough for him. Let's read a little more and find out what kind of woman would contain this man of God.

You'll remember that Elijah had asked her for a cup of water (during a drought), and then as she went, he added a request for a morsel of bread (in a famine). She replied, "*As the Lord* your God lives, I do not have bread, only a handful of flour in a bin, and a little oil in a jar; and see, I *am* gathering a couple of sticks that I may go in and prepare it for myself and my son, that we may eat it, and die" (1 Kings 17:12).

Both widows we've read about were empty, and this lady is truly at the end of her rope. When this little bit of oil and flour is gone, she fully expects there not to be another meal in their future. They'd eat what they had, and then they'd starve. But, as we've seen, God can do something incredible with those who are empty!

Though it may seem like a mistake to us, God had sent Elijah to the *perfect* person to contain what he carried. She had space for him—and therefore for God. How wonderful is it that God sent Elijah right into the enemy's heartland, where a woman was prepared to receive him? In the middle of a territory controlled by the wicked, a broken woman had a place for him. God had gone ahead and picked her out, and while she thought her brokenness made her worthless, it was her emptiness that set her up to receive what God was about to do! While still in her broken state, she had become a strategy for the Kingdom of Heaven, breaking the hold of the darkness.

Elijah's arrival interrupted this woman's life. She had a plan—not a very good one, but it was a plan. She was out doing her thing by gathering sticks to cook her last meal when God's sent man came along and asked for some of the very things she lacked: water and food. God seems to do this often because He is looking for those who will step

out in faith. She didn't know Elijah from Adam, but she responded in honor to him by going to get him a drink. Though she was broken, she had a willing heart but lacked resources.

Have you noticed that those who are often at the end of their rope and know it, respond best to the word of the Lord? **Those who don't recognize their emptiness are not open; they think they're full.** This woman realized she was empty, yet she still tried to honor the sent man of God.

Something happens when someone responds—when they turn from their plan to listen to the plan of God. They have an openness that the "full" do not, and that's something God can work with, no matter where they live or the condition of their lives.

That is good news, isn't it? Because that tells me He can use you and me!

More Than Survive

The widow of Zarephath knew she was running on empty. She would gather a few sticks, have a little fire, cook her little bit of food, and then settle in to die. I'm struck by the fact she was resolved to die. She'd been living with a survival mentality, but now she saw that had played out. There was nothing left for her (or so she thought).

This is the mindset of our age as well: Gather what you can to survive as long as possible. Preppers are teaching people how to make it if society collapses, yet I find it so odd that we see this in the church as well. You'll see people creating videos on religious TV saying that we need to stock up on food because we don't know what will happen. Get your food, gas, and cash—fill up those things, they say. They want us to hunker down as times get rough and survive until the Lord returns.

I hear people pray, "Lord, just come get us!" Many believers want God to rapture us all away from this place, but very few people seem to be sent men and women who are intent on taking as many with us

WE ARE CALLED TO OVERCOME DARKNESS AND ESTABLISH THE KINGDOM ON EARTH.

as we can! Why would we want to leave and abandon everyone else to Hell? Why does the church seem to want to get rescued from our difficulties instead of seeing the lost come to know the presence of the Almighty God?

Instead of an escapist eschatology, it's time we embrace bringing the Kingdom of Heaven *here* and through us. We have an idea in the church of leaving the Earth to go somewhere when we really should be bringing the presence of the King, the Kingdom of God, here. When we are focused on escaping the chaos and the darkness, we miss the very reason we were sent—to transform it. We are called to overcome darkness and establish the Kingdom on Earth.

Jesus prayed in Luke 11:2, *"Your Kingdom come . . . on earth as it is in heaven."* He also prayed in John 17, *"I do not pray for the world, but for those whom You have given Me, for they are Yours . . . . Holy Father, keep them through Your name, that they may be one as We are . . . . I do not pray that You should take them out of the world, but keep them from the evil one . . . . As You sent me into the world, I also have sent them into the world"* (vs. 9,11,15).

But it's like many churches are saying, "Let's just show up next Sunday, sing our songs, and listen to our messages . . . and then we'll die!"

We're hung up on praying for *sur*vival when God wants us to pray for *re*vival! God is looking for people He can send into the enemy's strongholds who are not as concerned with their comfort and convenience

as they are with transforming people to host the presence of God in their eternal souls.

A survival mindset is like a stronghold of Baal because it's all about self. When stuck in a survival mindset, we become highly self-consumed, self-contained, and self-focused. The enemy desires us to be so focused on ourselves and doing what we want that we miss the perspective of Heaven because we can't get our eyes off ourselves, our space, and our context. Then we miss what Heaven sees; and when we miss that, we miss out on Heaven's expectation. When we miss Heaven's expectation, there is no hope because righteous hope brings Heaven's move to Earth.

We cannot have hope or expect something from God when we're stuck on survival because we'll not expect anything different from the fate we've already assumed. So, how do we find hope if we're trapped in a survival mindset? We must discover godly hope.

Hebrews 11 teaches us that faith is the substance of things hoped for, and the evidence of things not seen, so righteous hope becomes faith—and faith is what changes the world. The hope in Hebrews 11 means "validated expectation" or "guarantee," not some wishful thinking. Whatever God says, you can *guarantee* it's going to happen. Our hope isn't in what we wish would happen; it's in what God says will happen and is faithful to perform!

When we live by hope rooted firmly in God's faithfulness, rather than focused on survival, we begin to be translators from Heaven to Earth. We become vessels to bring the approaching hope of Heaven's goodness to Earth as we get our attention off ourselves and onto Heaven, so we can see and believe with our faith until we see it manifest. If you have yet to see Heaven's goodness translated to Earth, you haven't "faithed" long enough!

Don't be discouraged if you haven't seen it manifested yet. Don't lose heart and give up! God's is faithful to His promises. We only need

to look at Scripture to see that He fulfills them in *His* timing. Look at how long it took Abraham to receive the promise or how long it took before Moses was ready to lead the people of Israel—decades! Yet we read that Abraham did not lose faith in God, even as his body withered.

God is sending His word, but He's looking for someone who will break free of survivalism and self-focus to look in hope at what the Kingdom of Heaven sees and respond to it with faith. The Bible tells us that when we respond to God in faith, He can do great moves on the Earth. But if we don't function by faith, it doesn't matter what word from Heaven is sent. Too many are under the misconception that if God said it, it would just happen. But the Bible tells us that even if the word is sent, it doesn't profit anything if it's not mixed with *faith* (see Hebrews 4:2). Heaven can send a word, but unless somebody on Earth is ready to receive it in faith, it will not produce. Remember, God works through people.

It's like ground waiting on a seed; God can send the seed, but He needs good soil for that seed to take root and grow into something fruitful. If there's no good ground full of the nutrients of faith for the word of Heaven, it won't produce anything. There must be somebody of faith to receive, somebody with hope. We cannot stay in a survivalist mentality and expect to produce much fruit for the Kingdom of God.

But if we accept God's invitation to faith and put our hope in Him, He will see the seeds of our faith sprout into great fruit, as Elijah and the widow would see firsthand. So, how do we do that? We prepare, just like this widow did.

CHAPTER 6:

DON'T FEAR, JUST PREPARE

IN THE PREVIOUS CHAPTER, we read how the Prophet Elijah came to a widow—seemingly the least likely person possible—to care for him during a time of famine. But God had a plan, and we have a great deal we can learn from this story today. Let's jump back into it to see how they handled this invitation from God and what He would do for His people because of their obedience.

Elijah asked the widow of Zarephath for a drink and then for a morsel of bread. He understood how frightening his request could be to her, but read the invitation to faith he gave this empty woman:

And Elijah said to her, 'Do not fear; go and do as you have said, but make me a small cake from it first, and bring it to me; and afterward make some for yourself and your son. For thus says the Lord God of Israel: "The bin of flour shall not be used up, nor shall the jar of oil run dry, until the day the Lord sends rain on the Earth."'

1 Kings 17:13-14

"Do not fear," he told her. He said, "Let's cancel that survivalist mentality right now." He needed to get her to repent (turn away) from that line of thinking that would keep her from pouring out because he knew if she kept thinking that way, she wouldn't be able to handle the word he'd brought.

The language used in this passage is interesting. The words "make me" can be translated as "to prepare." So, Elijah is telling her, "Don't fear; just prepare." Our fate will only change if we take our eyes off what we expect and begin to prepare for what God is going to do. If we want to break that survivalist mentality, we must quit looking at the end and start preparing right where we are. What may or may not happen down the road isn't in our power, but you can begin preparing today so you're ready when God begins to pour.

Even in the middle of our brokenness, depression, hurt, and discouragement; when you've been betrayed, kicked out, and abandoned; when you're sick, lonely, and broke—don't be afraid, prepare. God isn't done. Shift your thoughts from your negative focus onto God, and trust He will make a way where there seems to be no way. God has already been to your future! He's continually working things together for your good, and He's the Alpha and Omega, your beginning and your end. He is faithful and just, and His word will not return to Him void. It's not on you to do the miracle; it's on you to prepare with hope!

This widow's view of her future was bleak—she thought she was going to die. But instead, the word of the Lord came to her to prepare, and then God told her, through Elijah, how to do that.

God didn't just tell this widow to get ready; He promised her if she'd take what little she had and pour it out, He would fill it up. He wanted her to combine the little bit of flour and the little bit of oil she'd been holding onto, which is a faith-filled response to His word.

God knew what she had wasn't enough for what He was preparing to do, but if she'd give what little she had as an offering by pouring it

out and emptying herself, she would gain access to His presence. She would have to trust Him and have faith, but her leftovers in the hands of God would go as far as they needed it to go—the entire rest of the drought and famine.

When we pour out and deplete everything we've been holding onto, it breaks the hold of our past so God can take us into the future. For God to take us forward, we must release what is behind us. We prepare for what God has next by emptying ourselves as an offering.

God wants to send something to Earth through you and wants you to prepare, but let me act as the prophet here. You will stay stuck in the fate you thought was coming if you hold onto your survivalist mindset instead of stepping out in faith, which will then prevent God from working something through you. You've got to be willing to pour out what little you have. *That's* when God moves—not before.

We must empty ourselves of anything that keeps us in our survival mentality. Whatever you're holding onto, it's not worth it. God's future for you and those around you is bright, and the whole world can be blessed by your obedience to pour it out. We don't understand the magnitude of what emptying ourselves will bring to the Earth, but God does!

Personal Devotion

When God tells us to prepare, He often calls us to a place of personal devotion to Him. God is drawing us to the secret place where we can meet with Him to prepare for the moves He desires to do on the Earth. For the widow, that looked like her faith and obedience to make food—first for the prophet, and then for her family. Her obedience was an act of personal devotion, and it is the same for us.

"Preparing" looks like spending time with God and doing what He has told us to do. So why can that sometimes be so hard? I believe it's often because of strongholds in our lives. While the widow lived in a stronghold of Baal, we live in strongholds of things like secular humanism, which is the devotion to self. Just as surely as Heaven is pulling you toward personal devotion to God, there's a stronghold of the enemy that wants to pull you from it.

You've experienced it: Every single possible distraction seeks to keep you from spending time with God. When you sit down for a devotional time, your phone rings, the social media feed calls to you, or you quickly want to check the game score from last night. How often have you committed to spending time with God . . . only to make it a week or two before distractions and self-focus derail your good intentions? It's not difficult because you're foolish, lazy, or unable; a stronghold seeks to keep you from personal devotion to God because the enemy knows what happens when children of God prepare for His bright future by spending time with Him! Hell knows your pursuit of God will have a multiplied magnitude impact on the world.

Consider what happened with our first widow: Her response to God created great abundance. He didn't just fill her little jar; God poured out His oil into vessel after vessel until the house was filled and they could live off it. Similarly, the widow of Zarephath's faith-filled response would feed her household during a drought that lasted years.

GOD DOESN'T NEED EVERYBODY— HE NEEDS *YOU* TO BE WILLING AND EMPTY.

God didn't need an entire people to be empty so He could fill them; He didn't even need a town. God only needed a single widow to be willing to empty herself.

God doesn't need everybody—He needs *you* to be willing and empty.

God is so big; if He can find just one person, He can change the whole Earth!

He needs someone who will get out of the survival mindset to prepare for the outpouring of the Lord. Even if you're hurting, uncertain, or broken, it's okay; He specializes in working with broken people. He doesn't need the polished, sophisticated, or educated. God needs the sent, those who are willing to enter empty. He will pour out Himself through the broken, the contrite, and the empty who prepare for Him, even in the enemy's stronghold.

Sometimes, when we're in the enemy's stronghold, we wonder how God can use us. We wonder, "If God loves me, why did He leave me in such a desolate place? Why am I going through this? Why am I stuck here—in this situation, this location, this relationship?"

But God knows something we do not—that having someone on the *inside* is a huge advantage. The widow thought she was going to die, and we can think we're helpless victims trapped in the enemy's camp. Yet God sees us as an opportunity, situated behind enemy lines. We have a choice: We can see our situation as a negative fate, or we can see it as an opportunity for God to use us to change the world, starting right in the middle of the enemy's camp. This is where hope comes in.

You're not in a hopeless place, my friend. You're not helpless or stuck. You're primed and positioned! God has you right where you need to be, even if you're in the middle of the enemy's stronghold. When you let your brokenness empty you of everything holding you back, God can pour out blessings, hope, fruit, and light through you, even in the midst of darkness. Don't curse where you are; speak blessing over it. You may not be able to see it now, but God has positioned you to pour out His presence on the world!

Our job is to be "in the kitchen," spiritually speaking. We're just to be baking. It doesn't matter what's going on in the stronghold around us when we're where we're supposed to be and doing what God told us to do by preparing. It doesn't matter what's happening in your family, in your friend circle, in your town, or in your state. It doesn't matter what the politicians are doing in Washington, D.C., or what the state of the world may be; we're just to be baking biscuits—preparing. Everyone else can go crazy; it doesn't have any bearing on us and can't stop us from doing what God has called us to do, pouring ourselves out as an offering and preparing for the day when God makes a great move on the Earth.

This widow wasn't trying to change the world, she was baking biscuits. She was not locked in survival thinking, but willingly emptying out what she had so the Lord could multiply it and bring change to the Earth through her. Our job isn't to change the world, that's God's job. We're just to empty ourselves, so we're ready.

The widow was simply told to do one thing in obedience: Bake a cake. She went into her kitchen, and she prepared. She thought she was making a last meal, but really, her emptiness would yield results far beyond her, her son, and Elijah. God poured out on them in a small but vital way, providing for His people. Not only did they eat for the rest of the drought from her never-exhausted supply, but when the day of the Lord had come, Elijah went forth, and God poured out His presence on an entire *nation*.

Bread and Oil

We can read the Bible and see the result of the widow's obedience at a glance, but she had no such luxury. It was a complete act of obedient faith for her, yet unlike the widow with the vessels of oil from previous chapters, this story doesn't end with what God did for the widow or even Elijah. This story didn't end until there was an outpouring on all of Israel.

My friend, God isn't just interested in blessing you and your house—He wants to pour forth on the whole Earth!

The widow received the sent word of God. She obeyed the word, and we read that her flour and oil didn't run out until God was ready

to pour out rain over the nation. We, too, have the word of God and promises that if we empty ourselves, He will pour through us, and we know that God's word will not return void—it will always accomplish that for which He sends it.

Scripture tells us the widow's flour and oil didn't run out. Yet, it also tells us that we do not live by bread alone but by every word that proceeds from the mouth of God (see Deuteronomy 8:3). In the Bible, bread symbolizes the word (Jesus is also called both the Word and the Bread of Heaven), and oil represents the Holy Spirit. God will send us a word, which will keep coming until it has accomplished God's purpose, just like the widow's flour. When we chew on the bread of the word, we will *continue* to get a word from Heaven. The oil of anointing and the Spirit will continue to be an anointing on your life until there's an outpouring, but the outpouring we are waiting for is not physical rain, for which Israel was waiting. We are waiting for the latter rain of God's presence to be poured out upon the Earth.

The problem is that the church has largely missed the outpouring. We thought it would come from fasting, good music, or people running through the aisles. When I was growing up, they said it was a good service when the pastor didn't get to preach because "God was moving." But God only poured out His rain after the bread of the word, and the anointing oil of the Spirit had prepared the widow and Elijah. We need the bread of the word and the oil of the Spirit. I see a lot of gifts running rampant through the church, but for all the action, sometimes it doesn't seem like lives are changing, both at the individual level and in our culture. I believe this is partly because there's no word to match it and root it in the Earth. You don't get fruit without the root or establish a solid root without the word.

Remember, God's word never quits—it accomplishes exactly what He sent it to do. The anointing won't quit, and God is releasing a flow of His word and His anointing that won't run out until the Spirit reigns on the Earth. God promises, *"If My people who are called by My name will humble themselves, and pray and seek My face, and turn from their wicked ways, then I will hear from heaven, and will forgive their sin and heal their land"* (2 Chronicles 7:14). God is saying to us, "If my people will empty themselves and pray and seek my face, prepare with me in the secret place, I will pour out from Heaven and heal their land."

He doesn't need everyone to obey His message—He just needs a few. A few broken widows and obedient prophets are all it takes. I pray that describes me, and I hope it describes you too!

We look at the world and how big the need is, and it's overwhelming. But remember, meeting the world's needs is not our job; we must go into the kitchen and prepare. We realize our emptiness and then pour out the word and the Spirit He has given to us until the day of the Lord comes.

That's exactly what the widow did. We read, *"So she went away and did according to the word of Elijah; and she and he and her household ate for many days"* (1 Kings 17:15). She did the part God had for her, and her obedience and preparation to receive the sent word and then work the word she had, provided for her, her son, and Elijah. It also set the stage for one of the greatest miracles God performed through Elijah.

Let It Pour

In 1 Kings 18, we read the epic story of how Elijah faced off against the 450 prophets of Baal. King Ahab had led the people of Israel into idol worship, and they prayed to Baal for rain. All their prayers and all the efforts of Baal's prophets could produce no rain because it would not rain until the word of the Lord came.

And it came to pass, at the time of the offering of the evening sacrifice, that Elijah the prophet came near and said, "Lord God of Abraham, Isaac, and Israel, let it be known this day that You

*are God in Israel and I am Your servant, and that I have done all these things **at Your word**. Hear me, O Lord, hear me, that this people may know that You are the Lord God, and that You have turned their hearts back to You again."*

1 Kings 18:36-37 (emphasis mine)

God proved He was the one and only, the true God, when He then sent *fire from Heaven* to consume Elijah's sacrifice. The people saw the fire of God, and they knew Him for who He was—and Baal as a fraud. Before the end of 1 Kings 18, a tiny cloud the size of a man's hand quickly became a sky black with fat rain clouds that ended the drought and showered the land in refreshing rain.

As we are faithful to do the word we have, God will continue to supply words to us in due season. We prepare in the secret place during our personal pursuit of God, and we have no idea what God may do with that obedience. As it began to rain for the first time in years, do you think the widow knew how her obedience had prepared the stage for this great miracle?

A little woman at the end of her resources was willing to empty herself because of God's sent word. Will we?

You may think that your contribution is small, that God can't use someone as damaged or poor or alone as you are. But God is telling you to forget all of that—to forget how you think church should be done, what you believe your abilities are, and all your religious preconceptions. God is going to do something great and is going to pour out His presence on the world, but He doesn't need your abilities. He needs your *emptiness*, and when you give it to Him, God can pour Himself out over your life—and the lives of others around you.

The rain is coming! Are you empty to receive it?

CHAPTER 7:

FAITH TO ENTER EMPTY

IN THE PREVIOUS CHAPTERS, we saw that the word God sent to Elijah prompted a faith response from the widow of Zarephath right in the middle of the enemy's stronghold. God's word would not return void but accomplished exactly what He intended because the widow, God's chosen vessel, acted in radical obedience and provided for Elijah. Even though she was at the end of her rope, she made space for him—she was already empty and knew it. But God wanted more than survival for His people, and He used her obedience as the catalyst for a miracle that changed the entire land by breaking the drought. Her devotion to God opened the door for a mighty miracle to pour out onto her and thousands of others.

He wants to do the same through us.

God wants to rain His presence on us, but He is looking for people who, like this widow, have the faith to enter empty. But it can be difficult if you've had a life of hardship and disappointment, which we all have experienced. How do we find the faith to empty ourselves for God to fill?

Have you ever felt like Moses with the Red Sea before him and the armies of Egypt behind him? He had people looking to him for help, but he didn't even know what to tell them. Millions of people were crowded on the banks of the Red Sea, captivity or death coming up quickly behind them. It looked like the story of God's people would end before it had even really begun.

I've had moments like this where I've thought, "God, it's over." Circumstances happening to me, decisions that I've made, or symptoms within my body have all made me wonder. Would my ministry end like this—my *life*? What if I poured it all out before God . . . and He didn't come through? If you're honest, I'm sure you've also felt this way.

Yet, over and over, God has made a way, coming through against all odds, just as He did for Israel. If you're still reading this, you have not yet endured until death—and as long as there's still breath in our lungs, there's still time for God to work through us as empty vessels ready for Him to fill.

> **PROMISE LIES ON THE OTHER SIDE OF BEING EMPTY AND WILLING TO DO WHATEVER GOD TELLS US TO DO.**

With an impossible future and his past quickly catching up to him, Moses obeyed the word of the Lord and lifted his hands. As he did so, the waters of the Red Sea began to part.

Promise lies on the other side of being empty and willing to do whatever God tells us to do. He does His best work when there are no options left to us, and we surrender entirely to Him.

God is looking for people like Moses who will get out of the way, recognize their emptiness, and surrender to His supernatural power in their lives. He's looking for leaders who will take the

Body of Christ into promise. It won't be those who are eloquent in their speech or have a great plan. God is looking for those who know that when they reach the edge of a place with no tomorrow, their only choice is to lift their hands in surrender—who will empty themselves and be vessels for His presence.

I want to be one of them! Do you?

The Church Isn't Done

God has been merciful to the church for a long time, allowing us to continue with the bit of oil we have left. We haven't been as fruitful or productive as we could be if we were filled and overflowing with His presence, but we have survived.

Some think the church is done, it's all over, and we're irrelevant. They say the church is dying and has been for a long time. As I mentioned before, it's like we're the widow, gathering our sticks before we die. We're not influencing culture for God because we're just busy preparing for the end. In many ways, we've been the opposite of what God is— thriving and life-giving. And it's because all we have in the cupboard is a little bit of leftovers, just enough of His presence to survive.

BARE SURVIVAL IS NOT GOD'S GOAL FOR HIS CHURCH, THE BRIDE OF CHRIST.

I don't want to survive! I want to thrive in the life-giving presence of God's Spirit!

Bare survival is not God's goal for His church, the bride of Christ. Jesus came to give us abundant life, and we will be the vessels pouring that life into the world. Jesus' mere mention of the word "abundant" indicates that He is referring to a life of overflow here on Earth. Abundance in Heaven is unremarkable. Everything in Heaven is in abundance. His promise of abundant life is referencing yours and my life now, on Earth as it is in Heaven. We're at a crossroads, at an invitation. God's promises aren't just history. He has great plans for His people, and He's looking for those who will empty themselves.

Before the miraculous can take place, however, there's an invitation. Just like the widow of Zarephath, He is asking us a question and giving us a chance to participate in what He's doing on Earth. God loves us all individually, and His church as a whole, very much. Even though we haven't properly reflected who He is, He is extending an opportunity that will affect our destiny.

On one side, we have our way, all the things of this world filling us up with all the worthless stuff around us. This choice is that of self-focus and being self-absorbed, relying on ourselves to fill our vessels with what will satisfy us. And it never works, no matter how much we try to use the things of this world to fill our emptiness.

On the other side, God offers a vision of His presence and power moving on the Earth, an outpouring of His Spirit that changes lives and reshapes nations. This is the choice of focus on the Father and being absorbed with the Kingdom of God, where we rely on Him to fill us up with the only thing that will ever truly fulfill us—His presence. If we choose Him, we surrender personal control of our emptiness to God, elevating His will and ways above our own. It will require trust to have the faith to be empty, waiting on Him to fill us, but if we choose God, He will change the trajectory of our lives and bring us into His promise.

How will we respond?

Will We Accept the Invitation?

Let's return to Zarephath to tease a few more nuggets from this story of a woman who accepted God's invitation. Notice that Elijah warned the king and then headed into the wilderness before God directed him to an unknown widow who lived in a stronghold of the enemy. Through her, God would shift the future of a nation—if she accepted His invitation.

This woman was minding her own business, just like the church has been minding its business rather than being about the Father's. She wasn't thinking about oil and flour that never would run out or drought-ending rain; she was picking up sticks and preparing to die. The invitation God offered her would wreck her life.

Bring the prophet some water? That she could do. But he asked her to make a cake for the man of God *first*. She was barely surviving as it was! This would cost her everything she had left! How could she accept that invitation?

We want God to do miraculous signs and wonders, to show off supernaturally in our lives, but often, when we hear the invitation, we change our minds. God has a habit of breaking our religious mindsets by asking for the very things we're almost out of, urging us to empty ourselves.

Why does He do this? Because God knows what's on the other side of empty.

The invitation to empty ourselves doesn't seem wonderful and nice. It sounds like it'll take us to a dry, desert place—or even to our deaths. God often asks us to stop picking up sticks, which we feel we need to survive, and to offer to Him what little we have left.

It usually doesn't sound like a promise; it sounds like the end of everything.

The widow of Zarephath obeyed in a personal act of devotion. But how often are we paralyzed by fear, forfeiting God's promise to return to picking up sticks? How can we, as the Body of Christ, begin to see these invitations for what they are—opportunities. I believe it starts with prayer.

God Comes in Ways We Don't Expect

Have you ever received something far better than it initially seemed? Several years ago, I had a situation that God used to challenge my trust. I was single, living alone, in the infancy of my surrender to the Father and His call. I was broke—well, living by shallow paycheck to paycheck. I had a trailer that I let a friend borrow because he was getting married. Now mind you, I'm particular about my things. I take care of them and hold in my thoughts their monetary value.

So, he borrowed the trailer and then called me one afternoon and asked me when I had stopped by and taken my trailer back. I responded that I hadn't, and he began to poke at me for joking with him. I knew something was up. He proceeded to tell me that my trailer was gone. He had left it parked overnight at his old house and apparently somebody had stolen it.

At a previous time in my life, I probably would have lost it, but I heard the Lord say, "I want to see how you respond, how you handle him." I was in a situation where I needed money, and I had voiced that just a short time before on a phone call with my grandmother, and all I could think about with that trailer being stolen was not necessarily the trailer, but that it represented money to me. I needed the money more than the trailer.

On the ride home from work, after I had gotten the phone call from the friend, the Lord spoke to me again and said, "I want to know that you trust Me. You completely trust me, with *everything*." So, I decided I would indeed decide to trust Him with everything.

A couple of days later at my friend's wedding, a gentleman stopped me. He had heard the story from the groom, and God had awoken him during the night about it. God wanted him to talk with me about the trailer to get some information about it. Because of the nature of the wedding, we never were able to discuss it in detail. But about three weeks later, I got a check in the mail from the man for the exact amount that the trailer originally cost. He never even knew the type of trailer I had. God had permitted the situation in order to get me the money because I needed the money more than the trailer!

The old adage, "You can't judge a book by its cover," comes to mind. I had thought this situation would be a bad one, but as I trusted God, He turned it for my good!

The challenge with God's invitation is that it doesn't appear to be a promise; we often only see the apparent cost. He's a master of disguising His greatest blessings behind a veil of radical obedience. But I believe that if we pray and ask, "God, give me eyes to see and ears to hear," we will begin to see things more clearly—with His eyes.

God's invitations don't look tangibly fruitful or naturally enticing. His opportunity for a life, family, or nation to change by the power of the Holy Spirit will not look easy or fun. It won't look like an outpouring is coming, and it definitely won't look comfortable or convenient. God never sends a shift to the Earth that looks like what we think it will look like.

> **GOD'S INVITATIONS DON'T LOOK TANGIBLY FRUITFUL OR NATURALLY ENTICING.**

The Jews learned this firsthand with Jesus. They're *still* looking for the Messiah, because they expected Him to come dressed in robes and looking like royalty. Instead, God sent Jesus as a baby in a manger. The move of God arrived in a way the Jews never expected.

The widow of Zarephath's opportunity came looking like Elijah asking for what little she had left; it looked like a death sentence. God is making an invitation to us all that looks like emptying ourselves of

everything that comforts us, things on which we rely (even if they're unhealthy), and the baggage of this world. But probably most of all, God's invitation involves dying to our mindsets, and this dying hurts. When we die to self, we are parting with the only person we've ever known and been. But the promise is being genuinely filled, spiritual multiplication, and an overflow of His presence. It won't look like we expect, and it will require us to take a step of faith if we want to empty ourselves so God can fill us up.

God's invitation to us will look like that of both widows we've read about—being asked for what little we think we have left. Asking for all of us, not just part. Requesting that we empty ourselves out, leaving nothing left, and rely on Him completely. If you're already dry and feel dead in the desert, this can seem like too much. Our natural instincts kick in and tell us to gather all we can to survive, clutch what little we still have as a thin thread helping us cling to life. We hold onto the last things that keep us safe and whatever control we think we have.

That's why I pray that *"the eyes of your understanding being enlightened; that you may know what is the hope of His calling, what are the riches of the glory of His inheritance in the saints, and what is the exceeding greatness of His power toward us who believe, according to the working of His mighty power"* (Ephesians 1:18-20).

God's invitation to an increase of His presence is letting go of the rest of it. He's challenging us to pour out what's left. He'll keep inviting us until we release all control of the shape and direction of our lives to Him. That seems scary at first, but the moment we let go of it all and obey, we enter into a dimension we could never mentally prepare for.

We try to hold onto control because we think it gives us safety. But the moment we release control, we find ourselves in a greater place of authority because God wants to delegate His authority—the authority of the King of kings and Lord of lords—to us to steward. But first, we must acknowledge Jesus as our King.

When we hold onto control, we're making ourselves kings. We dream of kingly things for our lives, but we're living in peasant realms. We pour ourselves into the things we think we have control over, trying to elevate our lives, but the things of this world are worthless. God says He's put eternity in the hearts of men, but while we have kingly dreams, we lack the King's mindset, and our lives stay shallow when we don't surrender to His thoughts and ways. We cannot do this and hold onto what little we have left. If we want to walk in increase, we must get empty.

The Devil's Invitation

The devil is a liar, and he likes to tell us that what God's asking for will destroy us. This is why it's so important to have our spiritual eyes opened so we can understand the difference between how God works and how the enemy works.

We tend to think that anything "bad" that happens to us is an attack from the devil—even when the devil is nowhere around. Sometimes, the bad things occur because we're clinging to control. We can put ourselves in the wrong positions, blaming the enemy, yet our attempts to control everything and stay safe are often the very things that keep us stuck in survival.

The church can also try to stay in control, thinking we know what church should look like while we're actually operating in a spirit of religiosity. We believe we can control God and try to tell Him how, what, and when He can move. We can only meet once a week and have hour-long services; we can't speak the truth because it will offend. Jesus said *He* would build His church. When will we defer and surrender totally to the leading of the Holy Spirit who knows not only how to build His church but how to use His church to build and transform cities? Let us give ourselves to the "wait" that Jesus commanded for the coming of the Spirit, through our building of altars of surrender and repentance. We've been invited to a feast but are busy making excuses instead of entering the banquet.

There's only one prerequisite for sitting at the King's table: You. You are His offering. You are the living sacrifice. It is customary in kingdoms to never enter the presence of a King without an offering; a gift of honor. The only acceptable gift is you.

We're coached to bring something when we are guests in someone's house. Yet God's invitation to us requires nothing of us but being empty.

If we try to hold onto control and play it "safe," we miss out on all God wants for us. Where in Acts 2 did the early church play it safe, comfortable, or secure? The enemy wants us to live self-satisfied, self-successful, and self-full. He wants us to try to make our own influence, clout, and money.

The enemy constantly offers an invitation to be self-made. Look at the first thing he said to Eve in the Garden. He questioned God, then told her that if she'd step outside God's will, her eyes would be open, and she'd be like God. All the while, she was *already* like God!

Sometimes, we may think that Jesus doesn't understand what it's like to be at the end of His rope because He was God. But He was also fully man. So, how do we handle it when the devil offers his invitations?

In Luke 4:1-4 we read of Jesus fresh after His baptism: *"Then Jesus, being filled with the Holy Spirit, returned from the Jordan and was led by the Spirit into the wilderness, being tempted for forty days by the devil. And in those days He ate nothing, and afterward, when they had ended, He was hungry"* (Luke 4:1-2). (We'll return to His hunger later, so remember that how we handle hunger is pivotal to which invitation we'll accept.)

Here's the devil's invitation: *"And the devil said to Him, 'If You are the Son of God, command this stone to become bread'"* (Luke 4:3). Jesus was depleted. Forty days of fasting will rock your world! When it says He was "hungry," that was a massive understatement!

But Jesus understood what would happen if He entered His ministry empty and wasn't about to try to fill up any other way than His Father. We read, *"But Jesus answered him, saying, 'It is written, "Man shall not live by bread alone, but by every word of God"'"* (Luke 4:4).

In His depleted state, starving, faint, probably with a massive headache and all the other complications that come with such a prolonged fast, Jesus throws the enemy's invitation to be self-made right back in his face! The devil wanted Him to take matters into His own hands and to be *self*-filled, but God wanted His Son to be *Spirit*-filled!

And He wants that for all His other kids, too!

The enemy wants you to take what little you have in the cupboard and make yourself something to eat. Like Esau, he wants you to look at your present and sell out your future.

But Jesus knew the truth about hunger: The bread of this world alone doesn't fill us. Only God can truly fill us! The church will shift the world when we stop self-making our bread and stay empty and hungry until God fills us with His word and His Spirit.

The widow of Zarephath was about to make a little bread for herself and her son and then die, but God gave her an opportunity to change the world. She took it, and through her act of devotion, God poured out on the entire nation. What might He do through those who won't self-fill and wait for the Lord? I would love to see the Spirit of God fall afresh on His people and His church because we know what to do with our hunger as Jesus did!

Whenever we have an opportunity to self-make, and it doesn't go through the filter of being empty, it's not God. When they offer you a promotion, the first question is, "God, how do you want me to use this increase in influence and money?" Then ask yourself, "Am I building His Kingdom or mine?" You surrender your will, and you open

yourself to His. Jesus said, *"He who finds his life will lose it, and he who loses his life for My sake will find it"* (Matthew 10:39).

God is saying, "Don't make bread. Get empty! Don't self-fill. Let Me fill you!" He knows that is the only path to spiritual multiplication, and only by His Spirit can the Body of Christ accomplish the Great Commission and share the gospel all around the world.

CHAPTER 8:

GOD WANTS IT ALL

WHEN I SHARE ON ENTERING EMPTY, sometimes people ask me some very good questions. They may wonder, "How can I find myself on the cusp of being broke, and God still asks for more? I'm on my last legs. What more can He want?"

When we are asking questions like this, it means that we haven't searched our "house" enough. Until we are completely broken and contrite before God, we still have something left to pour out. God wants no indication of a self-sustained life. As long as there's still something in your jar and a little bit in your bin, God will ask you to pour it out—even if it means the only natural possibility from there is death.

"Why does God want me to die?" some may ask. God doesn't want you to die—He wants the self-reliant, self-sufficient, the one who relies on your own ways and understanding, to die. God wants to raise the new you, the Holy Spirit-empowered you, to abundant life! We never understand where God begins until we come to recognize where we end. God does not share credit, and He specializes in coming through in dead situations and raising them up in ways that we cannot take

credit for. He is inviting us to empty because God knows what is on the edge of happening, and only His Holy Spirit can do it.

That's why I encourage us to pray that God will open the eyes of our understanding and give us eyes to see and ears to hear so that we can become more aware of Heaven than we are of Earth. I want to be more sensitive to what God is seeing, saying, and doing than I am about what's going on around me in the natural.

Give It All

The widow was looking at a quicker death for her and her son by following the man of God's instructions and bringing him a morsel of bread. That may be the situation you're looking at. The Lord has said, "Give me a drink," and you're on the way to do it, when He adds, "Give Me more—give it all to Me."

God is wise; He knows what you have left in your house. David wrote that He searches the depths of the heart and knows all our ways. And, even more than we do, He knows what we have left—and how we're using it.

When Elijah asked the widow for a cake of bread, he told her not to fear. He knew that fear would quench her trust and rob her response. He understood what he was asking her to do, and he asked her to make him the bread *first*. This idea is important, and it bears out through Scripture. God is asking us to give Him everything, to empty ourselves out, and to do it *first*.

We've covered how destitute this woman's prospects looked. As a widow and a single mother in the middle of a drought in an agricultural society, she had no safety net and likely couldn't even trade anything with the neighbors (who may also not have had anything left). This woman had nothing else; using this little bit of flour and oil would make her *truly* empty.

In America, we rarely encounter anything remotely like this. Stop me if this sounds familiar: We say, "There's nothing to eat," when there is still food in our cupboards or refrigerator, because it's *not the food we crave.* And even if that food is exhausted, there are food banks and other programs if we look for them. We lack a frame of reference for exactly how destitute this woman was or what God was really asking of her: everything.

It makes me think of a conversation Jesus had with a rich man. The rich man wondered what he needed to do to enter the Kingdom of God, and Jesus told him to follow the commandments. The rich man replied he did that. We read, *"Then Jesus, looking at him, loved him, and said to him, 'One thing you lack: Go your way, sell whatever you have and give to the poor, and you will have treasure in heaven; and come, take up the cross, and follow Me.' But he was sad at this word, and went away sorrowful, for he had great possessions"* (Mark 10:21-22).

When Jesus asked the man to empty himself, he went away sad. I believe we can find America right here in these scriptures—we are rich, and we won't give it all away for God. We've come to church all our lives, filled pews, kept commandments, given things, and sung in the choir. But when God asks for it all, we balk and walk away. We often don't mind giving up "things" as long as we can keep "us."

> **WE OFTEN DON'T MIND GIVING UP "THINGS" AS LONG AS WE CAN KEEP "US."**

God exhausts us and breaks us, bringing us to the ends of ourselves. We may think our marriage, job, health, or finances are dying, but God is asking us, "Make Me a cake first. Take what little you have left, and give it to Me."

God is telling you to pour it all out because He's provoking a currency exchange. We often don't see what He's doing because we're looking at it in the natural. We think He'll trade dollars for dollars, but that's not how God works. Heaven wants to create a shift, and God takes what we give Him and exchanges the currency of this world for that which is eternal. He wants us to exchange trying to be rich in the worthless things of this world to be rich in spirit!

We think that if we give Him everything, we will have nothing left. That's what it looks like. Yet, when we empty ourselves, we get an increase. Our faith grows because God is replacing the things that will not last with those that are eternal. As our control diminishes, God's grace expands. As we let go, God takes over.

When I let go of my responses to my situations, God takes over with His responses to them. I give Him *responsibility*. If I trust Him to take over, I'm not relying on my own limited resources; all I must do is respond to the sound of His voice calling me to make Him a cake first.

It takes faith to do this. It takes faith to stare at your own breaking . . . and go ahead and break. It takes faith to be nearly empty and pour out what little remains before Him. It takes faith to bankrupt ourselves in the flesh so we can be rich in the accounts of the Spirit. But if we do this and step into His plan for us, we trade our material for spiritual. It takes being broken in the flesh to become rich in spirit. The only way we can have a transaction in the spirit is by the Spirit of God, so if we ever want to see a true move of God on the Earth, we must abandon the idea that we can self-make spiritual change so God can fill us with the only source that will empower us to live the life He dreams for us–His Holy Spirit.

The church has mistakenly thought we could coerce God with our activities. We keep trying to change God's mind while we hold onto the little bit of flour and oil in the cupboard, but Heaven's resources can only be transacted with Heaven's currency. We cannot provoke the

outpouring of Heaven unless we have embraced a Kingdom mindset and exchanged our little bit of leftovers for God's eternal supply.

New Faith for New Levels

Many people think they have faith, but sometimes it's faith for where we *were*–faith from last year or a different time. God wants to elevate us to new levels, but there's a catch with this: It costs more. Our salvation cost us nothing, but the promise will cost us *everything,* like this widow experienced. God wants it all, but He offers infinitely more if we trust Him!

Faith doesn't even activate until it's responding to empty. You can't call it faith until you're functioning on empty, having poured out what little you had left and put your future entirely in His hands.

Hebrews puts it so perfectly when it says, *"But without faith it is impossible to please Him, for he who comes to God must believe that He is, and that He is a rewarder of those who diligently seek Him"* (Hebrews 11:6). Why is it impossible? Without faith, we won't make the cake for God first. We'll hold onto it. But if we give God the first, the windows of Heaven will open and pour out for us such a blessing that there isn't room enough to contain it! Our response to empty activates the faith in our lives.

Why do we hold onto the little bit we have left? Fear and doubt entice us into thinking that God won't keep His word or be as good as He says. But God is trying to get us to see that He doesn't work like the world works. He doesn't require that we pay Him with interest; He eats the deficit. If we hand Him what little we have left, He will pour out Heaven on us!

God has something great in store for us, but it will take the most radical personal and corporate faith we've ever had. Just picture the sticks and nearly bare cupboards we have, and imagine that if God will pour out drought-ending rain upon the people of Elijah's day, what

does He want to do in our world now? Just picture the outpouring of His presence and Spirit taking over and flooding our world with revival!

God is looking for visionaries who will see what He is offering in the Spirit and have the faith to empty ourselves, step out, and watch Heaven take over. Can you see loved ones coming to Jesus? Can you picture a God-inspired culture change fanning our youth into flame? If you can dream it, it's because God is offering an invitation to see something new and fresh from His Spirit poured out on the Earth!

I recently received a text from an old high school classmate who was a staunch, professed atheist. He told me that something was going on in him, and I was the only person he knew to contact about it. I'm hungry to see God doing this in many lives as He draws people from every walk of life who are empty and ready for a fresh move of God!

Faith is the evidence of unseen things turning into seen things. God wants to develop it in us, because this is how He transacts the things from Heaven into our reality on Earth. But He doesn't just want people of vision; He wants people who will trust Him and transact faith in order to see the visions He's given us come to pass.

Earthly hope is fine, but I want to put my faith in God. I don't want to just touch a kingly dream that frustrates me because I lack the faith to see God pour out His Spirit—I want to see it come to pass!

How do we get rich in the accounts of faith so we can transact what God has dreamed for His people? By emptying our flesh accounts. Read Hebrews 11 and the "Hall of Faith" as God credited in faith accounts as righteous. God wants this for us, as well, and He is showing us that if we give it all to Him and hold nothing back, He will open the windows of Heaven!

For the Joy Set Before Him

We often don't see it this way, but Jesus had an invitation from God just like the ones He gives us. He was to pour Himself out as an

offering. He would die in His flesh, but by faith He knew He would be raised from death. Faith walks into a grave in order to be raised out of one—taking all of us with Him! For the joy set before Jesus, He endured the cross. He had faith that His Father would take that act of personal devotion and divinely multiply it, freeing us all of the chains of sin and death. It's the same type of invitation God gives us today.

I'm so thankful that God gave us examples to follow. Jesus went to the cross. The widow and her sons poured out their oil. The widow of Zarephath made Elijah a cake first. All of these acts of faith and so many others came before a great move of God, and He is offering you and me the same invitation He gave them.

He's saying, "Do not fear. Make Me a cake first, and I will show you that Heaven's resources are inexhaustible. I'll show you what I can do with the little bit you've been holding onto. Give it all to Me, empty yourself out, and watch Me! I will pour out like never before a new thing I am doing on the Earth, and your faith is your key to accepting my invitation to this move of God."

Will we surrender to Him? Will we give Him everything, even if it means there's nothing left for our next meal? We have a choice. We can hear this word but hold back in fear, or we can step out in radical obedience and see the miracles He desires to do on the Earth.

God has searched your house, my friend, and He knows what you have in the cupboard. He's seen the little bit you've got left, and He knows how much it will cost you—everything. But He's also assuring you, "Do not fear! Obey Me first and see what I can do!"

IT TAKES FAITH TO ENTER EMPTY.

His promise is *right here*, waiting to be accepted. It's an incredible invitation, and while it may at first appear to be the last thing you'll ever do, it's actually the

greatest purpose to which we can be called—transacting faith upon the Earth to see a move of God come.

It takes faith to enter empty, but let me remind you of this: You only need a little. Jesus told His disciples all they needed was a mustard seed's worth—just the tiniest grain of faith. He nurtured it and grew that faith within them, and He's doing the same in you. And He who began the good work is faithful to complete it.

Will you accept His invitation?

CHAPTER 9:

THE DEVIL DOESN'T WANT YOU EMPTY

GOD LOVES HAVING inside men and women willing to empty themselves so they can be filled with God's presence because He has chosen to do His works on the Earth *through* you and me. In the previous chapter, we looked at how important our devotion is because God uses our pursuit of Him to create a multiplied impact on the Earth. The widow of Zarephath could never have known how her obedient devotion would set the stage for the destruction of Baal's prophets or the drought-ending rain that followed.

The problem is that the enemy also sees the potential of our devotion, and that's why he works so hard to pull us away from intimate time spent with God. So, while God often uses us inside the enemy's stronghold to destroy it from within, the devil will do all he can to sway you to his way. He'll urge you to fill your life with things of this world, convincing you that they're vital; he'll try to persuade you that your devotion doesn't matter; and he'll distract you from focusing on God by trying to get your attention on *anything* else. Enemy worship doesn't look the way we often think. It's not blood and rituals and coarse language and rage. It's just disobedience, lack of surrender, denying God's invitations in order to satisfy self, protect self, or remain comfortable. This is a life of rebellion.

Why? Because he knows what God can do with even a single, submitted, contrite son or daughter who will empty themselves to be filled with God. I know because I lived this personally.

I've told you some of my story of how I began to live empty in my own life—how I lost my mentor, my health, and nearly my mind. While significant symptoms were wracking my body, I also recognized that it wasn't just a physical fight. I knew it was a very spiritual battle as well because the devil didn't want me empty—and he doesn't want you empty, either.

Looking the Devil in the Eyes

I love good barbeque. Where I live in South Carolina, we have some incredible barbeque sauces like sweet mustard and spicy vinegar and meat smoked with hickory or oak. One of my favorite restaurants is close to our home, and one night, we went out with a couple with whom we're friends. I was in the middle of my health battle, still trying to find my footing, and I was about to see what I was really up against. Some believers feel like faith looks like denial, but I think the devil does his best work in the dark, so I'm just going to be open with you as you read this.

You must understand this about our enemy: He doesn't fight fairly. He's an assassin, not a standup fighter, because he knows that he can't contend with the authority God has given His children. Instead, the devil comes at you sideways, attacking in ways we don't always see for what they are.

That's where I was in my fight. I was battling the symptoms, but I didn't always understand the nature of the battle. The enemy had gone

after my mind, and while I described some of the symptoms I experienced in my flesh, the attack on the battlefield of my mind was just as severe, if not worse. It got so bad it was driving me out of my mind! I thought I was losing it.

When I was a teenager, I had no self-esteem. I struggled a lot trying to find out who I was, which would lead to all kinds of other problems. While I never put a gun in my hand, I did experience suicidal thoughts as a teen. Would anyone miss me if I were gone? What kind of future did I have? I believe the enemy began to worm dark thoughts back into my mind. I was in misery, sick, and broken down. What would happen to me? I thought of my children, of them growing up without me. They were going to lose their dad, and I didn't know how to stop it. I don't usually think that way, but I was trapped in the enemy's stronghold. Just as Hell will fight to distract us in our times of personal devotion, the enemy was trying to take me down before I could learn what God wanted to teach me.

No one we were eating with that night had any clue what was happening inside me as I struggled to hold it together. The enemy was leading me down dark hallways in my mind, and here I was, a man of God and pastor, and thoughts of death were slithering in. It felt like I was in a dark tunnel, unable to see the light.

My youngest son had to use the restroom during dinner, so I went with him. As I dragged my body down the hall of the restaurant, it felt like walking in that dark tunnel. In the bathroom, at that moment, I felt the pull of death, of losing my mind. It felt like I was at a threshold; if I went any further with those thoughts, there would be no coming back.

It was like I was looking the devil in the eyes in that bathroom.

The doctors had prescribed me many medications because of the stress, depression, and anxiety I was experiencing. I had not yet filled those prescriptions. Now, I'm not at all against using medicine when it is appropriate, but I felt like the battle I was fighting wasn't physical,

it was spiritual, so I hadn't gotten them filled yet. As I was in that bathroom, feeling like I was looking into my enemy's eyes, I felt pulled to go around the corner to the pharmacy. This wasn't a normal pull or just a thought to fill my prescriptions, it was a fight for my mind, telling me, "Go get the pills. Take them, and everything will be better. You'll be fine. Go get them . . . ."

I was in a dark cloud when our friends came home with us to have fun and play a game. Instead, I *tried* to play because I felt like I was losing my mind the whole time. It was all I could do to hold it together. I'd had many dark nights like this, but this one may have been the worst. Yet, even in the stronghold of the enemy . . . God finds a way.

Battling against the dark thoughts the enemy was trying to use to destroy my mind was another thought: I should tell everyone what I was going through and get prayer. Our friends were also in the ministry, and I trusted them. But I felt ashamed of my weakness and of telling them exactly how bad it was.

I was struggling to empty myself of my pride. But I kept hearing, "Ask them to pray, ask them to pray . . . ."

It was time for pride to go! I can't remember whose idea it was, whether I asked them or they suggested it. All I can remember today is that we spent the next hour and a half on our faces on the floor before God crying out to Him. Today, I look at this as a saving moment for me.

That night was a watershed moment for me. The symptoms in my body didn't necessarily change, but a calmness and peace settled over me, and I was able to rest in God's presence and *sleep* that night. It's amazing how incredible it is to get a good night's sleep when you can't do that simple, refreshing thing.

The devil doesn't want you empty. He knows what can happen when we leave this world's baggage behind and forsake all others but God. He fears what will happen if you lay down your pride, agenda, expectations, and anything else that keeps you from emptying yourself.

The enemy knows what the Lord can do with just one sold-out believer who is willing to, like Paul, call it all loss. In Philippians 3:8, Paul writes, *"Yet indeed I also count all things loss for the excellence of the knowledge of Christ Jesus my Lord, for whom I have suffered the loss of all things, and count them as rubbish, that I may gain Christ."*

I don't know what the Lord will call you to as a first step on your road. For our first widow, she gathered vessels and then shut the door. For the second, she obeyed and baked bread with the last of her flour and oil. For me, I had to humble myself and ask for prayer.

I want you to take a few moments, during which you're going to put this book down and come before the Lord in prayer. Perhaps, like me, you may want to pray on your face before Him, which is my way of showing reverence. Maybe you need to get alone with your Bible, free of distractions, and brew up some coffee or tea. I suggest bringing a pad of paper so you can leave your phone behind. Whatever a time of meaningful devotion looks like for you, I want you to go into the secret place and pray for God to show you what your first step toward emptiness looks like. Ask Him to show you what you've filled your life with, and then ask Him how to lay it down before Him. As He reveals things, write them down. Take as long as you need to, and don't rush. When you return, we will examine what it means to say yes to God.

Cling to Yes

I hope the Lord showed you your first steps, but if you haven't received anything yet, I suggest you try again after the next chapter when we'll begin talking about *how* we enter empty in more practical terms. But before we do that, I want to spend a little time on something important because if we don't cover this now, the enemy may try to discourage you before you even begin.

The subtle deceptions and ferocious attacks of the enemy are a war. **Never forget he hates God's people, and he will stop at nothing to**

get us to quit. The enemy has challenged me with everything to get me to quit; to challenge my yes. Everything I was experiencing in that bathroom and all the spiritual and physical battles I fought were just that—an effort to get me to quit. It wasn't the first time and won't be the last, but we do not face our foe alone. James wrote, *"Therefore submit to God. Resist the devil and he will flee from you. Draw near to God and He will draw near to you. Cleanse your hands, you sinners; and purify your hearts, you double-minded"* (James 4:7-8).

While you may wish I had some grand strategy to teach you for defeating the enemy's attacks, what God taught me in those dark days was incredibly simple: Cling to Him. I felt called by God for years before I answered it, but I found a surprising strength for my foundation in hanging on to my "yes" to God. When I did sell out to God, I went all-in. Though I didn't have the words for it at the time, I let go of the things that held me back from saying yes to the high calling of Jesus. In essence, I had emptied myself to respond to the call He'd placed on my life, which gave me a solid foundation.

God sent His word—He called me out from among the things of this world—and I gave Him my word in return. This has been the central root of the tree that kept me grounded and that keeps me coming back to God over and over to do my assignment on this Earth. The enemy has tried to destroy me by surrounding my life with addiction, those dark thoughts I had as a teen, all kinds of sin and foolishness, and rejection after rejection.

But it didn't work! I now know beyond all doubt that I cannot do it alone. I know that programs, doctrines, education, and tactics cannot sustain me and that my only hope is Jesus Christ. His grace is sufficient for me; I know that intimately because I've lived it.

For all of the enemy's attempts to destroy me, I have learned the powerful lesson that I cannot defeat him with my own strength. But

when I empty myself and rely exclusively on God—not God *and* anything else—I find the strength to take the next step He has before me.

I shared with you that I came from a broken home wracked with addictions, but that was nowhere near as dangerous a tool against me as rejection from within the church. I felt God calling me to Him between my first and second years in college, but I ran from God for *years.*

I started my college career at Clemson University, but it wasn't a good experience. After my first year in college, I was running a tractor in the bush, hogging a forty-four-acre field by myself. No one else was around, just me and my headphones. I was working when something incredible happened, that has not happened again since, I heard God as an *audible* voice. He said, "You know what I have for you to do."

I stopped the tractor and looked around to see who'd spoken, but I was the only one in that field. I put the tractor back in gear, turned up my headphones, and pretended I hadn't heard a voice alone in the middle of a field. But He said again, "You know what I have for you to do." I'll never forget it!

I'd sensed God's call on my life even before this time. I had always attended church growing up, and I can look back and see the grace of God on my life. I remember that when I was in sixth or seventh grade, I spent six months or a year carrying my Bible with me every day and saying I was going to be a preacher. Even in utero, my Uncle Lane Sargent prayed over me prophetically. He had laid his hand on my mother's stomach and said, "There's something on this child."

My dad kept me in church and in that atmosphere, but that time in the field was the first I'd heard it directly from God. While I knew what God meant when He said that, I wasn't ready to surrender my life. I fought it, or rather, I ran from God. I never got into drugs and alcohol, but that was more about my passion for football, rather than strong convictions. I didn't want to do anything that could ruin my chances to play ball.

I did try to fill up with things other than God. I tried to get the affirmation and esteem I needed from my many relationships. Still, eventually, I began to see that I could be with as many women in a day as possible, but I'd still have to come home and look myself in the mirror.

Even after I met my wife, Serena, I was terrible—we got engaged *three* times, but I kept ruining it! At one point, I had done so much damage to our relationship we didn't talk for two years. I was desperately trying to fill the void in my life with destructive things that didn't satisfy me while running from the only One who could fill it. I ended up running from God and from my calling for six and a half long years.

I was downstairs working out in the home gym when it all began to catch up to me. I was tired of trying to outrun the call of God on my life as well as all the hurt and brokenness I carried with me. I had a moment like the prodigal son, where I came to my senses and decided to go home to the Father. In that home gym, God showed me something—my life, like a picture book. He showed me the various things I'd gone through, and it was the first time in my life that I felt totally valued and affirmed. I felt like I heard Him whisper to my heart, "I allowed you to go through some things that would've broken another person because I trusted you to carry them."

I felt ten feet tall and bulletproof! God trusted me!

Yet it also broke me. I experienced that broken spirit we discussed earlier—not damaged and destroyed, but that contrite heart and repentance. I threw myself at God's feet in surrender because nothing in life had offered me the kind of affirmation and satisfaction that I had experienced with God. I had tried to fill up with women, football, work, and so many other things, but it left me with a life without substance or meaning. Nothing and no one could make me feel like I was worth anything; my life had no purpose. None of the other things could fill me up because everything else was meaningless.

Serena and I had been engaged twice previously—two engagements that, ultimately, I helped destroy because I hadn't stopped running. We had gone two years without talking, and everything looked as though we would never speak again. In the middle of that period in my life, God spoke to me and said, "Don't worry about the mission, the ministry, the marriage, etc. Just give Me the man (myself). If you'll let Me shape the man, the rest will come out of that." So, I tried my best to do what He asked—give Him myself. When Serena finally did see me again, she could tell something was different. Maybe not perfect, but different.

We actually reconnected when my grandfather was in a battle for his life, fighting cancer. He lived about an hour and a half from me, and I felt this urge to go pray and lay hands on him. For some reason, I felt led to ask her to go. Mind you, we had not talked in quite a while, but she actually agreed to go with me. We went and prayed, and I laid hands on my grandfather in prayer and helped do some things to care for him while we were there. One was to move him from his bed to his recliner before I left because he was uncomfortable. He actually passed away where I laid him, less than eighteen hours later. I don't know what it was about that trip, but that's where we reconnected, and in just six months, we were finally married.

It Didn't Get Easy Just Because I Stopped Running

So, the church people I came to at first knew me from before, and knew the kind of person I had been. And when I began to share that I felt called to ministry, they could only see the Jason I had been. They didn't trust that God had done a work in my life, maybe partly because they hadn't seen the fruit yet.

But mostly, it's because I had been a fool. I grew up in church; it's where I met my wife, Serena. Her family moved up from Florida, and her dad was on staff at our church. When they moved up from Florida, her brother and I hit it off quickly. We hung out together a good bit. I was over at their house often, but Serena was a little younger, so we didn't really pay attention to each other at that point. A couple of years went by, and things picked up just from being in the general group together. We went on some dates and group dates, but at the time, all I cared about was playing football and chasing women.

I was a freshman in college at this point, and this is where my running began. So I went after all kinds of women and had my eyes set on football. I transferred to Troy University in Alabama, and Serena stayed pretty connected to me, but I treated her more or less as a part of the game when I returned home. It wasn't until after I came back from college that we really began something more serious.

So the man they all saw was the Jason who ruined his relationship with Serena—not once, but multiple times. I didn't know what to do. I felt this draw to God, not just to relationship but ministry, yet the only people I knew were those I'd negatively biased with my sinful, foolish behavior. My past unfaithfulness was hindering me in many ways, but all I wanted was a spiritual father to show me the way to answer the call of God.

Even though God straightened my life out, the shadow of it continued to haunt me. I found that many spiritual leaders don't understand fathering or discipling. They don't know what to do, so they distance themselves from it. They didn't know how to take a broken young man and turn that contrite heart onto the path of discipleship, so they didn't do anything with me at all. I'd experienced many rejections by that point in my life, but this felt different.

It was an invitation to quit.

But God had a plan. Interestingly enough, my mother—with whom I have a very difficult and spotty relationship—began going to a church in a different denomination than what I'd grown up in, where she met a pastor. She told him I was called to ministry, and he wanted to talk

THE DEVIL DOESN'T WANT YOU EMPTY

to me. I'd never been to his church, but I went to that appointment one night and shared that God was calling me to go into ministry and become a pastor.

"I want to help you," he answered when I told him I wanted to have my own church someday. And he did help me—he gave me opportunities, and I threw myself into serving at his church and loving people wholeheartedly. Ultimately, I spent around ten years faithfully serving God under this man's leadership, becoming friends and confidants. We never even had a single cross word with each other!

The enemy learns our weaknesses, and again, he sought to discourage me. After all those years of serving, during which I never hid that one day I wanted to be the lead pastor at a church of my own, I finally felt I *had* to move on. In fact, I'd been feeling that way for three years and had been shoving it down. So I was incredibly discouraged and rejected when this man with whom I'd been so close reacted negatively to me when I finally resigned to follow God's call.

I can tell you from experience that few things will fill up your life like bitterness and rejection can. We can easily bank on those things, hoarding them like something precious when, in fact, they're poisonous. We can gather them together, and they will fill us with toxins that will eat you away from the inside.

When this man reacted so poorly to my leaving, I had a choice to make: Would I hold onto that bitterness and pain, or would I let it go? This was a powerful early lesson on emptying myself out so God could fill me.

In addition, I also learned I'd filled my life with something else God had to clean out later (remember the sepsis He spoke about to me?). Where once I'd filled my life with sports or women, now I was filling my life with pursuing my calling. I felt my assignment gave me value, and it also brought me the affirmation I so dearly craved. It's easy to love the things that love us back and to fill up on them. I often used to

say that I loved football because it loved me back, and I filled my life with it until injury took it from me at twenty-two. I'd given everything I had to football for years, and now I was giving everything to God— but did I need the affirmation a little too much? I derived my sense of value and purpose from it.

As I present it like that, I'm sure you have no problem seeing that even filling my life up with God's gifts isn't the same as filling it up with *God*. But I didn't know that at the time, and it took the dark journey of my sickness to truly teach me how to empty myself of that, as well.

Looking back, I can now see that the difficult times after my family and I left that church to start our ministry were emptying as well. I knew I was called; I knew God had given me gifts. I had nowhere to use them, and no doors opened for us. I'd resisted the urge for three years after the time I was to be sent out, and finally, God had gotten fed up with me staying stagnant. Yet, when He moved us, it did not result in immediate success.

It was into the wilderness.

CHAPTER 10:

AN EMPTY CHURCH

"I'M ABOUT TO CARRY YOU . . . ."

God said this to me while I was still working for the pastor who helped me get started in ministry. I felt the need to leave and follow God's call, to build leaders and be a spiritual father to those growing in the ministry, but in the years before we left the church where I'd served to follow God, He told me, "I'm about to carry you to the place where leaders die."

Encouraging, right?

He continued, "I'm doing this so you will know how to return to that place and rescue others from it. I'm about to carry you into a wilderness, and you will think I'm not there. You will not hear from Me or see Me. I need to know that you'll keep reaching to Me when you don't feel Me reaching back."

The season that followed—as we left our paycheck behind to follow God—was a preview of the years I would spend learning to trust God while so sick. (In fact, I am sure this is where God established something in me: that clinging to Him was my only option.)

God told me it was time to go, but like Abraham, He didn't tell me *where* we were going. It was just time to leave. So, we did—we followed God out into the wilderness.

I left my position as an associate pastor in August of 2013, and we didn't end up founding our church, Rejuvenate, until April 2015. Those years were a no man's land, where no one helped us, and we had to learn to rely solely on God. It was a profound time of God emptying us of many things!

I sent forty-four letters to churches and denominations I'd been connected to. Not one response came back. My paycheck had come from my position as an associate pastor, so I also had no steady income for nearly three years. But we still had a house payment and needed food, gas, and all the rest. What to do?

Trust God!

Then, another baby was on the way, and Serena wanted to stay home with the kids instead of work. What to do?

Trust God!

Those years were rough, but it was also a time when I saw the hand of God moving often. It's one thing when you cling to the call on your life while God is obviously with you, communing with you, and demonstrating His greatness daily. It's an entirely different issue when you're in the place leaders go to die, wandering a wilderness, and just grateful for the manna that sustains you for that day.

Everyone around me questioned my sanity. My relatives asked what we were thinking, and Serena didn't always know how to respond. She and I had some very frank talks because we had to face the realities of life, but in critical strategic moments, she affirmed me, "Keep pushing because this is what you're made for."

She wanted to stay home with our kids, but she was making just enough at her job to cover insurance and childcare. Then, when we

had our youngest son, it was time. "I'm quitting," she told me, "I'm coming home."

I had no idea how to make that happen, but this is when He finally picked to make His move.

In It Together

I'm so thankful that God put us on the same page. Before we stepped out of our previous ministry, we went on a trip to a conference, and the speaker talked about Jonah getting thrown overboard. I was so stressed out, feeling the effects of the years we'd spent in our wilderness. As I listened to the message, I just began to weep. Some people were with us, and I didn't want them to see their leader ugly crying. They didn't know how hard this had been on us, and I wasn't ready to reveal it.

But this was the moment I knew that Serena also had the vision: She stood up and walked beside me to shield me as I cried. She sat me down in a chair, and I just wept. But I knew at that moment that she had gotten it and heard from God.

There's something truly dangerous about a couple willing to surrender it all together to be filled with God!

We felt we were to be in ministry, but it didn't seem like we had a path forward. I went to church planting conferences, but there they told me we'd never make it. They advised me to stop, give it a year, and build up some church-planting money before I came back to them later.

At the conference, they painted a picture of how they thought the church should work—a bumper, three songs, a sermon bumper, and a twenty-five-minute sermon. I stood up in front of perhaps four hundred people and asked, "So, when do we listen to God? When do we let Him move?"

I called Serena and told her that 80 percent of the business stuff was pretty good, but I felt like I had that down. I had tears in my eyes as I told her, "I can't sell myself for fifty thousand dollars to start a church. I can't sell what God has sent me to do. He'll find a way to do it!"

I don't have a formal education in theology, and I never went to seminary. Nobody taught me except the Holy Spirit. I was a football player, and I have drive and intensity. But at least God didn't have to empty me of my educated religious misconceptions because I didn't have them!

My life speaks to being empty, because I wasn't filled up with something before God got to me. I didn't have any preconceptions. We didn't have a big ministry, and nobody sent us off with fifty founding families and a year's salary (and all the baggage that would come with them). When we finally did start our church, it wasn't an established church building; nobody was in it. We didn't even have a Bible study group meeting first. Everything we did started from empty.

Rejuvenated

In March of 2014, Serena and I first thought of starting our church in a school, like all the other church plants do. But initially, the school board wouldn't let us because we hadn't gotten our federal paperwork back—which would take another six months minimum. We had a bank account but no money. We didn't know what to do.

I felt God put it on my heart to go to a nearby town and drive around. We ended up at this mall, and while my wife and daughter headed to Claire's, my middle child, Braylon, began running around in the center of the mall (he was maybe three at the time). As I slowly followed his insane energy, I saw that one of the properties in the mall was vacant.

Suddenly, I felt drawn to that property, and my wheels started spinning. "God, is this why I'm here?" I prayed. I felt confirmation—this was why we were there. "A mall?" I asked.

"A mall," God confirmed in my heart.

I told Serena about it as we walked into the parking lot and shared that I thought I was supposed to call and talk to the property manager about that empty space. When I called the next day, they didn't know what to do with me! No one had ever asked them if a church could meet in a mall, and they had several thousand properties nationwide.

"I'm going to have to talk to the high-up people," the guy I talked to finished. He asked me to send him materials that showed we were legit, and after talking to the higher-ups, he called me the next day. "They're telling me to show you the property. Let's meet in the mall."

We started at one end of the mall when we met, and this guy showed me the various open properties. On the last one he showed me, the Lord whispered, "This is home."

I told the property manager, "I know this doesn't make sense to you because you're a business guy, but this is where we're going to be. Go ahead and figure out whatever numbers you need to." I looked around and said again, "This is where we're supposed to be."

Later, in prayer, I felt God give me the number we would pay. Now, remember, we have *no money* in the bank. All we had was our emptiness. But God was already teaching us what He can do with nothing!

When the property manager got back to me, he gave me three times the number God had given me. Of course, I felt defeated. "What do I do, Lord?" I prayed.

I just kept feeling that God had given me a number, and I needed to stick with it. So, I emailed them the number He'd provided me on a Friday. We went to the coast that weekend, but I had a reply on Monday when I checked my email. The property manager said, "They've accepted your offer."

We were so excited! Yet, even that number was more than we had in the bank, which was nothing, and they needed a reply. How could I commit to something when I didn't have the money for it? I kept feeling that if we just had three months' rent, the presence of God would work out the details. We just had to get started.

That following weekend, I was scheduled to preach two services at a Baptist church. I didn't say anything about the church we were planting, but as I closed that morning, I told the congregation that my wife and I were in the middle of doing something we really felt like God wanted us to do and asked them to pray for us. That evening, I spoke to some people who were connected to us and shared what had happened that week with the mall. I shared the situation we were in, with having to commit with no money.

A gentleman said, "I just feel like if you just had, I don't know, three months' rent just to get down there . . . ."

I got up, walked across the floor, and said, "Man, if I had three months' rent right now, I would call him tomorrow and tell him yes."

Nothing happened that night. I didn't walk out with a fat check. But I had faith that God would perform the sent word He had given us. I went to our PO Box that following Wednesday to get the mail. Inside was a letter from a man who attended the church I preached at that Sunday. In it, he shared that he'd heard me preach twice and believed in God's call on our lives. They were committed to their church, but he wrote, "We want to be a part of what you're doing. My wife and I want to sow into you."

Inside the letter was a check—for three months' rent. I had never shared the exact amount, but it was the same amount of money we needed!

I called my wife, screaming so much she thought something had happened, like I'd been in a wreck!

We had a building!

It had been a lingerie store and a wine shop before that. But now, it would be a church following after God's heart. Not beholden to any denomination or tradition, we started our church empty with no preconceptions.

. . . no preconceptions, and no *people*!

Every day, I would drive down to our building in tears because I was going to a church building without the CHURCH (*we* are the church)! I didn't have anything to do yet, so I would go into the building and pray. I'd sit out front at a pub table in the opening that faced the mall, or I'd be in the back of our little sanctuary on my face before God. You could say that this was also a time of empty, and I would pray in that emptiness every day.

We began doing a Bible study every other Sunday night, and a few people started to connect. Only a couple of people came at first, but God began to bring them bit by bit. Mall-o-ween meant an opportunity to stand there and hand out candy, and I think we got two families that day.

People came in, and we even had the chance to connect with the mall management. Within three months, God allowed us to connect with one woman who had been the mall secretary for decades and is currently the mall manager as I write this. Her daughter was struggling with addiction. One day, I had the chance to pray for her about a heavy issue her daughter faced. They wanted to get into a particular in-house rehab facility that was very expensive. They didn't have the money for it, but the facility offered a scholarship once a year. We prayed for a way for her daughter to get into the facility.

Three days later, they got a letter telling them they would be the recipient of the scholarship! God made a way for this family, and she has always dealt with us favorably. When this woman was hungry and open, God touched her life.

Earlier in the book, I said that God has invited the expected guests, but they haven't come. So, He's inviting those from the highways and the hedges—the forgotten, the hopeless, the lost. They're desperate, and desperate people recognize what's important. They see how empty their lives are, and they become open for God to do incredible things. If only all His children would recognize that He is all we need!

Out of the Wilderness

We had faced opposition from every corner when starting in the ministry, but God had made way for us, too. God had carried us through the wilderness where leaders went to die, and He'd brought us out on the other side.

The devil didn't want us to enter ministry empty, but he couldn't stop God's plan. And while our rough time of questions was difficult, I now wouldn't change it for anything because it taught me that God was all I needed. If I'd gotten connected with one of those ministries and they'd sent me out with money, people, and chairs, we could give them credit; the same is true for the pastor I worked with for so long.

But God made sure we had *nothing* when we started—nothing but Him. He'd begun teaching us to cling to Him—a lesson I'd desperately need in the most challenging fight of my life. But just like Caleb (see Joshua 14:11), I have never fought in my own strength. It's always been His.

When we launched, Rejuvenate Church was the only known church in an active mall. As I write this, we still meet in the mall. We now have five properties that canvas the mall, covering over 30,000 square feet, with the vision to take over the entire mall, *and* we have also helped father another church in a mall in the lower part of our state. God took our emptiness, and He began to pour out His Spirit.

CHAPTER 11:

CARRYING THE WORD

SOMETIMES WHEN I SHARE about entering empty, people wonder if this means they can never do anything fun or casual again. That's not what I'm saying. I don't expect that after reading this, you will become a missionary in Siberia or never watch another football game.

No one in history has been more filled with God's presence than Jesus. He only said and did what the Father told Him, yet I think it's interesting that Jesus started His earthly ministry at a *party*—a wedding. This wedding was His debut venue, and I want to look at the symbolism this wedding has for our lives and our relationship with God.

It's no coincidence that Jesus began His ministry at a wedding. While a marriage was happening in the physical world, a wedding between the Bridegroom (Jesus) and His bride (the church, us) was beginning in the spiritual realm.

Weddings have a symbolic meaning, as they involve the joining of two people into a covenant. God established the Earth, which we can see to reflect the spiritual which we cannot see, and weddings are a picture for all of us who need illustrations to learn. Jesus talked in parables because that's what we can grasp, and marriages are parables for joining Jesus and the church. They're pictures of the love, sacrifice, and intimacy God desires to have with His people.

In all honesty, I wouldn't say I like doing weddings much anymore, because fewer and fewer people place value on marriage. Many couples don't take their marriages seriously or see what they represent, so it's discouraging when I take it more seriously than they do. We're not just putting rings on each other and moving in together to save on expenses; it's a serious covenant agreement representing the covenant between Christ and the church.

Traditional Jewish weddings such as the one we'll read about were beautiful, and rich with meaning. The father would pay a price for the bride, showing that the covenant requires a cost. The groom would go to his father's house, where he'd prepare a chamber for them to be together, and then he'd listen for the father to call him when it was time for him and his bride to be joined together.

The bride would prepare by being cleansed in preparation for intimacy. She'd get all cleaned up, do her hair and all the rest, and dress in her finest, waiting for her groom to come. Neither the bride nor the groom would know the exact time the call would come, so they had to stay alert and aware.

GOD WILL BRING THE OUTPOURING; WE ONLY NEED TO PREPARE.

When the father sent word to the groom to come for his bride, he was preceded by a shout. This told the bride her groom was on the way. Soon, they would consummate their relationship and be bonded, not as two but now as one. It was rich with meaning and beauty and deserved a joyful celebration!

As we look at the Bible from Matthew to Revelation, we can see that the time between Jesus' ascension and Revelation 13 is this preparation time. But our Bridegroom is coming again—with a shout! He has gone ahead to prepare a place for us that we may be with Him, and our job here is simple: prepare.

There's a word for us in this because, as I mentioned earlier in the book, our job is to get ready. God will bring the outpouring; we only need to prepare. I believe the church is moving into a time of cleansing and preparation for a greater level of intimacy. God desires to be closer to us, to be intimately connected and joined together—not as two, but as *one*.

Intimacy with God always produces fruit, a multiplication. It's important that we prepare because our personal devotion will yield greater intimacy and life-changing fruit that will pour out on the world. And if we cast off all that holds us back and be washed with the water of the word, we will be ready—and empty, cleansed of the stuff of this world like a purified bride before her wedding. Just like we wouldn't go to our earthly wedding all sweaty and dirty from cleaning the house or working out at the gym, we don't want to go into intimacy with God still soiled by this world.

God desires to pour Himself into you. Will you allow Him to wash and cleanse you so that you can be a bride without spot or wrinkle for the marriage with the Lamb of God?

Enter the Celebration Empty

You'll remember that when God gave me this message about entering empty, He also used the example of the parable of the wedding feast. The wedding guests got their invitations, but for one reason or another, none of them showed up. They were too busy and distracted by the things of life to attend, so the ruler throwing the celebration had his servants go out into the countryside to find everyone who was not

usually invited—the broken, the down-and-out, the hiding, the scared, the overlooked, and the discounted. They entered the highways and hedges to find people to join the celebration.

God showed me church people are the usual guests who didn't show up. Those of the world He is drawing to Himself are the guests who realized that they were broke and destitute, who saw their lives as empty, and had nothing to hold them back from coming to the party. One group knows how to dress, talk, and walk the walk, but despite their appearance, they are missing the point. They rejected the invitation because their lives were full of other things.

In contrast, the empty ones didn't look the part. They didn't know how to wear their church mask or talk our jargon; they came just as they were without pretense. Which group did the master of the feast celebrate? It certainly wasn't the ones who were invited but rejected him!

All of Heaven is gearing up for the wedding celebration of the Lamb. He has gone ahead to prepare a place for us in His Father's house. That means it's time to get cleaned up. We can't make ourselves clean (our best is filthy rags), but we can be washed in the water of the word and be cleansed. This is the emptying process, getting ready for an incredible level of intimacy. We can't expect a greater celebration of God's presence on the Earth until the church decides it wants more intimacy with our Bridegroom.

We won't be ready for the bridal chamber and the greater intimacy coming unless we're ready to be empty, cleansed, and purified. We even need to be emptied of our old religious thinking, programs, and ways—anything that doesn't look like what God intended.

But this isn't just all serious work. A wedding party is a perfect illustration for us because if all events on this Earth were just frivolous wastes of time, why would Jesus have attended with His disciples? A wedding is a serious representation on Earth of a spiritual truth, but it's also a *celebration*. Jesus understood that we would not be disconnected from the world—we would be in it, but not (*full*) of it.

Let's look at His first miracle together and see what God has to teach us about our relationship with Him through a wedding party, a party on the brink of disaster.

Jesus Goes to a Party

We read the story of the wedding in Cana in John's Gospel. Let's take it one piece at a time. *"On the third day there was a wedding in Cana of Galilee, and the mother of Jesus was there. Now both Jesus and His disciples were invited to the wedding. And when they ran out of wine, the mother of Jesus said to Him, 'They have no wine'"* (John 2:1-3).

Many scholars believe that Mary was the one invited to the wedding, and it was possibly a relative of hers. Jesus wasn't the celebrated guest; He was more like Mary's plus-one (plus disciples) because He was relatively unknown at this point in time.

I find a lot of similarities here between the wedding and the modern church. There's a celebration of the masses, and if you look around a little, you can probably find Jesus there. Only one person (Mary) shows up with the Word. He doesn't show up with everybody, because while many may know Him as the carpenter's son, not everybody knows He's the King of kings. Jesus wants everyone to be part of the celebration and for everyone to know Him intimately, but only a few do. Many are invited, and they're looking for the one who comes with the Word. The one who brings Jesus changes the game for everybody else.

Mary saw the problem—they'd run out of wine. Running out of wine at an event like this would've been a great embarrassment to those throwing the party. It showed they weren't prepared. Running out of wine mid-party shows their hospitality wasn't very good, and hospitality was very important in those days. Everyone showed up at this party expecting to have a special time, yet the hosts now didn't have enough for their guests.

Imagine throwing a wedding, but you're not ready. Stop for a moment and picture it—the guests are showing up, but everything is not in order. You're missing something important. How would you feel? The guests are milling around uncertainly, and at some point, it could ruin the whole celebration and send everyone home early. Everyone will remember this for years . . . We read it with a passive eye, but if you try to put yourself in the situation, it starts to feel more uncomfortable. This will be a memorable wedding, all right—but for now, it's for all the wrong reasons.

In the Bible, wine represents life and blessing, the blood of Jesus, and the Holy Spirit; also, free wine can represent God's gracious gift to us. Coming back to the symbolism with the church, churches are running out of wine. We have not adequately counted the cost of the party and prepared accordingly, and now, as guests show up, they're finding God's church dry. This is supposed to be a celebration, but everyone wonders, "Whose problem is this?" Wine also represents Jesus' blood, so what does it say that the church is dry without the wine of His presence?

We're arguably in the most critical time in history, and the church is dry. Somebody must show up with the Word. Someone must welcome the flow of the Spirit of God rather than go through the motions of a celebration without the wine of God's presence to give us life, vitality, joy, blessing, and prosperity.

The invitations have already been sent. The wedding is happening. Who will take responsibility to prepare for what God is going to do on the Earth and not be left embarrassed and ashamed? We're trying to celebrate without the wine of His presence at this critical hour. We have filled ourselves and our churches with programs and activities,

but we're dry without the Spirit of Jesus, and we won't be ready for what He is about to release if we do not get filled up with His presence.

Thank God, someone showed up with the Word—Mary thought to bring Jesus with her. What looked like it would be the most embarrassing moment of the wedding party suddenly had hope: Jesus was there! Everything changes when Jesus enters the room; the same is true for us.

A Test

Mary brought the Word with her, but as we read, we'll see that Jesus needed to know something first. It says, *"Jesus said to her, 'Woman, what does your concern have to do with Me? My hour has not yet come.'"* (John 2:4-4).

If you don't read that correctly, you might think Mary got rejected. After all, He just called his mom "woman"! First, Jesus wasn't rude to His mother; the term would perhaps be better translated as "dear woman" or "dear one." But was this a rejection, or was it a test of her faith?

Remember, God doesn't need everyone to move on the Earth; He needs *someone* to call upon the name of Jesus because He always has the answer no matter the question! Mary was that person, and she didn't hesitate at all. She didn't call a prayer meeting about what to do, didn't send for an evangelist to get everyone fired up, and didn't put the problem in the church bulletin. She was in a close relationship with Jesus because she was living with the Word from Heaven.

We don't need more services, programs, albums, or websites. We don't need focus groups or conferences. All we need to do is turn to the One who has the wine and say, "I don't have any wine."

Yet He replied that His time had not yet come. Why? He already had fasted and been in the wilderness, filled with the fullness of the Spirit, and had disciples. It sure seems like His time is ripe.

God asks revealing questions of us, not because He doesn't know the answer, but because He wants to see how we'll respond. Jesus wasn't interested in what was happening with anyone else at the wedding; it was just Mary and Him. But when we have a conversation with God and respond in faith, there will be a transaction from Heaven to Earth. If we can live by faith and not by sight, trusting Him, it doesn't make any difference what the situation is.

The solution is always the same: Jesus!

Mary came with the Word, even if no one else at the party had it. He wanted to know, "Do you still believe?" and that is why He answered the way He did.

I love Mary's faith as she responded: *"His mother said to the servants, 'Whatever He says to you, do it'"* (John 2:5). We can learn from this because we often try to shoulder the weight of the responsibility, but Mary *sidestepped* it. She was only there to make a connection between the Word with her and the problem. She handed it off to Jesus in faith, which is precisely what we're to do. Mary could easily have doubted after hearing Jesus' response. "Is it not His time? Does this really matter to Jesus?" But Mary reacted with faith, not letting the enemy rob her confidence in Jesus.

What would happen if we responded to our problems by simply introducing them to Jesus and saying, "Whatever He says, do it"? When we put the responsibility on Jesus, we open our lives to an extremely powerful transaction between Heaven and Earth that takes us out of the spotlight and makes it about God and His faithfulness.

Jesus was challenging Mary's faith. To Him, Mary was the most important guest at this wedding, and the whole passage shows that this wasn't really about the wedding—it was about Jesus and Mary. It was about her faith as she trusted Him with her problem.

How did she know? Jesus hadn't done anything miraculous yet. She'd watched Him build a table, just like Joseph did. He'd made

cabinets and drawers, but He hadn't raised the dead, healed the sick, or walked on water yet. How did she live with such unshakable confidence in the Word?

It's because although she hadn't seen anything miraculous from Jesus yet, she had been carrying a word from Heaven before He was even born! After all, an angel had appeared to her and told her she'd become pregnant, though she was a virgin, and that she'd give birth to the Messiah. After shepherds came to the manger where baby Jesus lay and told them about the angel choir they'd seen lighting up the sky, we read, *"But Mary kept all these things and pondered them in her heart"* (Luke 2:19).

Mary held onto the word and didn't let the fact that thirty years had passed affect her faith. We must also hold onto our promises and keep ourselves motivated for when we see them manifest. It's easy to get excited when God does something and our emotions are high, but if it doesn't happen in a week or two, we start to lose motivation. If God doesn't do it in *our* timing, how often do we question Him?

Mary had been cherishing those things in her heart and carrying a word from Heaven for *thirty years*, knowing a moment was coming when the Word would be released on the Earth. She was ready to trust Jesus with her problem—no matter what.

Are we?

Let's take a look at how Jesus responded to this opportunity in the next chapter as we see what a wedding teaches us about entering empty.

CHAPTER 12:

TASTE AND SEE

EARLIER, WE SAW HOW the widow of Zarephath received the sent word and prepared. God poured out, but not just for her. Her preparation set the stage for God to move on a whole nation, bringing them back to Him. But as we saw in the previous chapter, a time is coming when the world will need to know who you have *with* you.

Mary brought the Word to a wedding celebration in Cana because she lived with Heaven's expectation, not a survival mindset. Mary was navigating the situation the way Heaven would. The other guests saw a problem, and that the party would end in embarrassment; Mary saw an *opportunity*. She recognized that no one else had the power to do anything except the One she brought, who could change it all for everybody.

Do we see our problems that way? Do we see the empty wine pitchers of our lives as a tragedy, or do we see them as *opportunities* for God to pour out and show off? Mary understood that God was going to do great things, which gave her a sense of expectation, and that's the way I want to live as well. Let's take a look at what this story of a wedding has to do with entering empty.

Obedience Leads to Empty

Remember from the last chapter that Mary had handed the problem off to Jesus because she had faith in the Word she had brought with her. She told the servants to do whatever He told them to do. Now, let's change gears and look at the next piece of this story, how Jesus responded to her faith.

We read, *"Now there were set there six waterpots of stone, according to the manner of purification of the Jews, containing twenty or thirty gallons apiece. Jesus said to them, 'Fill the waterpots with water.' And they filled them up to the brim"* (John 2:6-7).

You must read between the lines here a little, and I want to briefly key in on one thing because it is also a metaphor for us. The six stone waterpots contained twenty or thirty gallons each—contained, present tense. They had something in them, so they had to be emptied before the servants could fill them with water. Somebody had to take those large, heavy pots and empty out whatever was in them so that they could be filled up.

RADICAL OBEDIENCE LEADS TO EMPTY VESSELS.

Remember Mary's words: *"Whatever He says to you, do it."* When they did it, it led to empty vessels. Radical obedience leads to empty vessels, which sets the stage for God to pour out.

Throughout this book, I've been saying that we need to enter empty, and I promised to dig deeper into how that works. You may have tried kneeling at the altar or have been in your prayer time, throwing your emotions at God, only to find that you still feel as burdened and weighted down as you did when you started. Aren't we supposed to cast our cares on God, for He's our burden-bearer?

We tell Him, "God, here's what I'm facing. Here's how I feel, what's happened to me, and what I've gone through," hoping that this will help unburden us.

I'm all for telling God how we feel and talking with Him as someone does a friend, but this is not how we get *empty*. That's baring your soul. But this passage gives us an indication of how we genuinely empty ourselves.

We all have many different things happening in our lives; our vessels are filled with all sorts of stuff. I'm going to give you one thing I have found that works for everyone who wants to empty themselves out so they can be filled with God, regardless of their circumstances: Listen to God, and when He tells you something, do it—*obey*.

Mary told the servants to follow Jesus' directions, but they probably didn't know Him. And He was telling them to empty those heavy pitchers, then fill them with water. They had to be wondering how that would solve the wine problem. Was He just making extra work for them? The key was, *they did it.*

Their obedience set the stage for God to do something, and the same is true for us.

When we respond with radical obedience and do what He tells us to do, it leads to emptiness. Obeying God involves the sacrifice of self. Proverbs 3:5-6 says, *"Trust in the Lord with all your heart, and lean not on your own understanding; in all your ways acknowledge Him, and He shall direct your paths."*

OBEYING GOD INVOLVES THE SACRIFICE OF SELF.

So many people pray and give God their pain, give Him their past, and give Him their doubt, but they miss a vital step. We can cry all day long, pouring out our hearts before God—and

as soon as we're done, we can pick our emotions back up again when we leave.

But will we *obey* what He tells us to do? Will we obey and empty out the little oil we have? Will we get busy preparing in the kitchen? Will we empty our dirty vessels out so they can be filled with water, even though we need wine?

If we learn how to respond to God with radical obedience, we will lay down our pride, emptying ourselves as broken, contrite daughters and sons of God. Empty vessels no longer choose our way over His. Instead, obedient servants humble themselves.

We arrive at empty through *obedience*.

Listening and Obeying Brings Purification

So often, we claim we cannot obey because we don't know what we are to do. We must choose to *listen* to God carefully if we want to get empty.

There would have been a lot of noise at the party. People were everywhere, laughing, joking, talking, singing, and, if they were anything like modern families, arguing. The master of the party was giving orders, but the servants didn't need to listen to any of that–they needed to hear the Word. One master started this party, but a different Master would finish it.

We face a lot of voices in our world today. Noises and instructions come from everywhere. So, to whom will you listen? Will you listen to the master who started the party without enough wine, or will you listen to the One through whom miracles come?

For these servants, listening and obeying meant first emptying water jars used for ceremonial purification. (Notice that Jesus didn't have them bring the jars used for wine.) Following Him meant doing something different than the Jewish religious practice, which involved a lot of ceremonial washing because they were constantly getting dirty, dusty, and contaminated by the world. They wore sandals, and they stepped in unmentionable things all the time. They got dusty from the blowing winds, and there weren't showers around.

They had a religious practice for getting ceremonially cleansed, but Jesus was doing something new. Consider this: These pots for purification would have had the remnants from all that washing. These weren't clean, empty pots just sitting around, waiting for Jesus to fill them with wine. They were contaminated, corrupt.

I love this because you and I were once dirty vessels. Jesus took the most unclean things in the building and did something utterly miraculous with them. He *chose* the *dirty* vessels, the ones no one would think to put wine in.

He chose you and me.

But before He fills us up, He must first empty us out. He knows that if He first cleans us from the inside, the outside will be clean, too. We read in 2 Timothy 2:20-21, *"But in a great house there are not only vessels of gold and silver, but also of wood and clay, some for honor and some for dishonor. Therefore if anyone cleanses himself from the latter, he will be a vessel for honor, sanctified and useful for the Master, prepared for every good work."*

We've filled our lives with our own righteousness, with the best we can do—but it's filthy. Our religious activities don't make us clean; we must empty ourselves of our attempts to try to make ourselves *look* clean and valuable because it's all just filthy rags to God. But if we're empty, Jesus can fill us with His living water. Dirty and clean cannot be in the same vessel; they can't share space. This is why we must pour out first, because if dirty water is still in the bottom of our vessel, it will contaminate the clean water Jesus pours into us.

It's time to pour out what you thought you had to work with. It's time to empty your giftings, your expectations, your ways, and your

mindsets. It's time to make room and eliminate anything that would contaminate all God wants to pour into your life—don't trust in it, don't put your faith in it.

Only when we're empty can He fill us with His presence. He wants to fill you with His Spirit to the very brim!

Walk It Out

Let's look at what obedience looks like. They had to empty the pots and fill them with water, but then Jesus asked them to walk it out. We read, *"And He said to them, 'Draw some out now, and take it to the master of the feast.' And they took it"* (John 2:8).

You might think that after they filled the water pots, Jesus walked among the pots, dipping His finger in them and turning them into wine—and *then* they drew the water out and walked it to the master. But that's not how it happened; when they put the tasting cup in, *it was still water*. This means that at some point between them responding in obedience by dipping the cup into the water (the Holy Spirit) and walking it out (by faith) to the master of the feast, it became wine.

They had to trust what Jesus said and walk by faith and not by sight, because by sight, it was still water! While they were walking, they could have said, "Wait! It's not purple yet! I'm not taking this pot of water to the master of the feast!" How many believers fall down here with the very provision they need *in their hands*, but they doubt the Word?

All the while, God is asking us, "Will you trust Me?"

What had started out as just another wedding party had become a faith-building debut and a collision between Heaven and Earth.

Jesus once told a parable of two sons (see Matthew 21:28–32). The father told them to work in the vineyard, but the first said he wouldn't go, yet regretted it and went. His brother said he would go, but he didn't obey. Which did the will of the father? The first did. Even if we have to squeeze our eyes shut as we walk out our faith, all that matters is that we respond to the Spirit with *obedience*. It may not be easy, and it doesn't have to look pretty or sound all religious, just so long as we do as He has said and not be hearers of the word only but doers. When we do what God tells us, we are emptying ourselves out so that He can fill us.

It Only Takes a Taste

Imagine being the servant bringing a cup you just dipped in a ceremonial washing pot full of water. In obedience, you're walking among the wedding guests (who are starting to murmur that they're out of wine) with a cup of water. You'd have no way of knowing what Jesus could do since He hadn't done any miracles yet. You just had this Man's word to go on.

Let's see how it worked out:

When the master of the feast had tasted the water that was made wine, and did not know where it came from (but the servants who had drawn the water knew), the master of the feast called the bridegroom. And he said to him, "Every man at the beginning sets out the good wine, and when the guests have well drunk, then the inferior. You have kept the good wine until now!"

John 2:9-10

The master just needed a single taste to know this was the best wine ever! David wrote in the Psalms, *"Oh, taste and see that the Lord is good; Blessed is the man who trusts in Him!"* (Psalms 34:8).

It only takes a single taste!

Previously, we saw that one woman and her sons could receive what God poured out to set them free of bondage and provide for them on what was left. We noticed that another obedient woman, who went into the kitchen to prepare, set the stage for one of the greatest miracles in Elijah's ministry. Now, one woman showed up to a party with the Word of God, and she and a few obedient servants who understood the power of being empty changed everyone else's experience at the wedding and set the stage for Jesus' earthly ministry.

Throughout Scripture, wine was a significant part of covenants. It's no accident that Jesus served His disciples the first communion with bread and wine before His crucifixion. This was not a wine to get drunk (they drank watered wine anyway because it helped kill the impurities in their water); it was the wine that symbolized covenant.

While many know *of* Jesus, few are in covenant with Him—even in the church. Those who think they know Jesus because they've heard of Him believe that they have what they need, but they have not filled their lives with Jesus—they've filled them with other things. So, God is calling those hungry for something (they may not even know what) to the party because they are willing to come and admit their emptiness. They are the water pitchers, the vessels that may be dirty but open to filling, rather than those who think they have God but are full of the wrong things.

GOD WILL POUR OUT HIS SPIRIT ON THOSE WHO MAKE SPACE FOR HIM.

Culture may believe the best of the church is behind us, but I am prophetically declaring that those who hunger and thirst for righteousness will be filled. Whether they come from within the church or come to God from the bars and gutters, God will pour out His Spirit on those who make space for Him. On the other side of empty, we will find the most unique, authentic, and pure wine of the Spirit the world has ever tasted!

The church's best days are not behind us. There's new wine about to pour, and it will be the best yet, just as the wine at the wedding in Cana was the best of the party. The master of that wedding must've thought it would end terribly, but instead, it was the best party he'd ever been part of because Jesus had entered the scene, ushering in the outpouring of the Spirit.

This outpouring won't come through the old traditions. It won't come through just anybody. It will come through those who have decided to empty their dirty water pots, those rejected by religion, those thought too dirty or disqualified.

It will come through us.

Perhaps you've thought, "How could Jesus choose a dirty vessel like me?" But regardless of your past, you are not disqualified. God will use any willing vessel, anyone willing to empty themselves out through obedience to be filled by His Spirit.

If you're willing, pray this prayer with me: "God, I'm listening. I am willing to be empty so you can fill me with your Spirit. Tell me what You want me to do and where You want me to go. Please tell me how I can obey and respond. Tell me what You want me to pour out. Tell me how to prepare. Tell me how to pour, what to pour, and when to pour. Tell me who to give it to, when to give it to them, and where they are, so I can pour out your Spirit."

The world is going to taste and see God's goodness, and it will come through a bride purified and cleansed by the Word. My friend, that is you and me.

CHAPTER 13:

FULL BUT DEADLY

IN THE PREVIOUS CHAPTER, we saw that God chooses to work with all kinds of vessels—even the dirtiest ones—that are empty and ready for Him to fill. We can eagerly hunger for the outpouring of the Holy Spirit, but He won't come through old traditions. He'll come to those who enter empty and choose not to fill up on the worthless riches of this world.

When we make room for God, we prepare for the power of God. There aren't too many places this is clearer than in the life of Mary, Jesus' mother. After hearing that she would be filled with the presence of God and give birth to the Messiah, she sang a prophetic song that included these lines: *"He has put down the mighty from their thrones, and exalted the lowly. He has filled the hungry with good things, and the rich He has sent away empty"* (Luke 1:52-53).

Interestingly, the translation for the word "hungry" here means those who are empty, and the translation of the word "good" means that which originates from God and is empowered by Him. I take this to mean that those who are empty have made space to be filled with what originates from God and are empowered by Him, but those

WE'RE TO BE PRESENCE- FILLED, PRESENCE- CENTERED, AND PRESENCE- LED.

who trust in the riches of this world will be disappointed.

Yet, sometimes, we can get lost in the things *of* God instead of getting lost in our love for Him. We get lost in having the things, the blessings of God, but this scripture tells us that we will be *filled* by what's empowered by Him. God created the Tree of Knowledge, and Genesis tells us it was both pleasing and good. But God wasn't in it. Much of our church culture today seems good and pleasing, but God isn't in it. Much of what occupies our lives may seem good and pleasing, but the truth is that God isn't in it. Cities, regions, and nations aren't going to change if we continue to structure our approach to ministry or our lives by what seems relevant, packs seats, promotes advancement, or is popular; we are going to transform by *presence*. We can no longer allow our church structures and cultures to be determined by growth conferences and metrics or even comparison to the latest booming church in attendance. Instead, we're to be presence-filled, presence-centered, and presence-led. If we continue to put butts in seats but not power in people, we will not see lives transformed and cities redeemed. God will build *His* church by His Spirit.

In the church, we've been okay with associating with the things of God, but at some point, we must lock in on what is empowered by Him. We have missed out on effectiveness for the Kingdom because the church can be "rich" in religious practices and mindsets, but we have not learned how to empty ourselves so we can be filled with what He empowers.

Some time ago, I celebrated the life of a man who greatly impacted me and many others. For the first time in my life, I saw a man who lived empty but empowered by God. He lived a life poured out, filled up privately and poured out publicly. He lived with an authentic devotion to the Father and his call to be a father to many—a life lived as a living sacrifice to God and given away to others. He was full of love and power. He could make you feel like you were the only one in the room by relationship and yet could change the atmosphere of a room by assignment. You could hear from God when he was speaking and also know the love of the Father when he was up close. Much like Jesus, he could sit with three, dine with twelve, or speak to thousands around the world, and in every capacity, the presence of God was there. It was amazing to see the reach we can have when we live a life empowered by God instead of just functioning in the things of God. The church has many leaders who operate in the things of God, but I saw a man who impacted nations and generations because he was willing to live empowered by God through emptiness.

I want to live that kind of life! I don't want to be wordy; I want to be weighty. I don't want to be gifted; I want to be glorified. I don't know about you, but I want to walk empowered, and there is a key to that I'd like to teach you.

Rich or Hungry?

Mary's song shows us that God wants to fill the hungry and empty and empower them with His presence, but it confirms that those who trust in their riches will be sent away empty-handed. That promise conflicts with our culture because we widely believe that the rich have everything they want or need, while the poor should be pitied. The truth is that those who are rich in the things of this life are deceived;

they aren't really wealthy at all, and the poor and empty are the ones whom God can fill because there's nothing in the way. True riches are not measured by money but by empty lives full of faith. Faith is the currency of the Kingdom of God. Whether you have money or not, a life empty of selfish pursuits but full of faith is the measure of richness.

Our culture, its ideology, and everything it presents to us is designed to make us desire to be rich and have things. Just turn on the TV and look at the commercials! The spirit of the age, the devil, understands how to manipulate, deceive, and corrupt something that's not bad . . . and to use it for our destruction. Having cars, houses, and dollars in your bank account isn't inherently bad. What's terrible is that the world is trying to get you to live with a mindset focused on riches and filling up with the things of this world. We live enticed, marketed, and bought by the opportunities that feed the insecurities of our flesh and our soul because our spirits are in deficit.

You see, the devil knows what happens when we live our lives with a desire to be empty. Our hunger shakes him! He's afraid because the Bible tells us that God empowers those who are hungry. But those who trust in their riches will find it hard to enter the Kingdom of God, because the riches of this world are worthless.

Part of the spiritual conflict of living in an abundantly blessed nation is that we often don't know how to remain in pursuit of God. We don't know what it means to stay hungry because we have many other things to fill us up.

I recently had the chance to speak with two men from Africa. They had been living in the United States for over a decade. We began discussing God's presence and the Spirit's move in Africa. There, many don't have the ability to become rich, so they know how to pursue God out of hunger. People hunger for the Kingdom. They are desperate for a move of God, for the presence of God, because He is their hope. They are not short on salvations; miracles happen in plenty because they live a life in jungle prayer—prayers rooted in cries of desperation because they have nothing else to look to. Either God moves or nothing. They weep when they receive a Bible because of the scarcity there, and they honor and give thanks that they're holding God's Word.

In China, the government won't let them become rich, yet God is moving powerfully. Believers in these nations and others have a greater level of spiritual empowerment than what we typically experience in America because here, we have everything at our fingertips, and we are not hungry since we have so many other alternatives.

Yet God has given America political power and authority on a world stage, and we have sometimes used that power to impact the world for Jesus. I was in a conversation with a few Jamaican gentlemen about the apathy of America in posture toward the Father. They were asking what the problem was in America. God immediately prompted my spirit for me to say, "We're too rich. We are the rich young ruler in the Gospels. We're able to keep the general commands and maintain the religious narrative but are greatly unwilling to sell off what possesses us in order to follow Him in total surrender." He wants us empty! The enemy is hard at work trying to capture our minds. He knows if we can ever break free from being filled with the riches of this world and begin to empty ourselves and steward His power for the Kingdom, the church will change the world.

Changing the world seems so big, but it begins very small—in your life, home, church. Can you imagine what God could do with people who bring hunger for Him into their daily lives?

The devil has been doing an excellent job of making us addicted to responding naturally to spiritual provocations. When we're hurting or depressed, we eat. When we're broken down, we spend. When we're lonely, we seek the wrong kind of comfort. When we're broken, we medicate. We try to fill the emptiness with *anything*—usually, anything *except* what is spiritually substantial.

We want to control that feeling of emptiness, but God wants us empty to break our attempts at control! We try to fill our lives full of riches, but God wants us *whole*. Unless we grasp that He is trying to show us the worthlessness of this world's riches, we will completely miss and disregard the spiritual opportunities of God happening in our lives.

Are you in a dry place, a desert? Do you feel like your life is meaningless? Do you feel frustrated? The very reason we find ourselves in these empty places is so that we can recognize the grace of God trying to draw us in so He can fill us with the only thing that matters—

Himself. It's time to lay down our attempts to take control with sleep, spending, drugs, sex, or whatever you do to try to fill the places He's trying to break open.

God has a better plan. He knows being full of this world will leave us feeling worthless. He has a different path for you and me: to learn to live hungry.

A Hungry Church

What would happen to us, the church, if we learned to live continually desiring God's presence—not satisfied with anything less?

That's what broke out in Acts. When the disciples asked the resurrected Jesus if He would now establish an earthly kingdom (showing their thinking was still locked into this world), He told them to be focused somewhere else: *"But you shall receive power when the Holy Spirit has come upon you; and you shall be witnesses to Me in Jerusalem, and in all Judea and Samaria, and to the end of the earth"* (Acts 1:8).

The disciples had a burning desire for God after the Holy Spirit's empowerment at Pentecost. They no longer wanted to be rich in the things of this world; they wanted to be hungry—and whole. Look at how it affected them:

All the believers devoted themselves to the apostles' teaching, and to fellowship, and to sharing in meals (including the Lord's Supper), and to prayer. A deep sense of awe came over them all, and the apostles performed many miraculous signs and wonders. And all the believers met together in one place and shared everything they had. They sold their property and possessions and shared the money with those in need.

Acts 2:42-45 (NLT)

I'm not telling you to quit your job, sell your house, and live in a shipping container. But God has given us the ability, through the empowerment and indwelling of the Holy Spirit, to empty ourselves out—to stop filling up on the worthless riches of this world—so we can instead stay hungry for what only God can give us.

The believers in Acts laid down their attempts to take authority over their empty feelings and instead decided to live whole. God isn't trying to keep you from filling your needs or leave you depressed; He's trying to help you understand that nothing on this Earth will fill you in the meaningful way you crave. He will permit things to happen in your life that make you feel empty so that you desire to encounter Him and become whole.

When God draws you to those places, those valleys, and deserts, He will powerfully meet you if you embrace that emptiness. He will pour into you, filling you in a way the world never could. The question is, will you go willingly or reluctantly?

Empty versus Emptying

I have three kids, and let me tell you, there's a difference between them doing what they know to do and me "helping" them do what they know to do. They know not to fill up on junk food before dinner, but I may have to remind them if they forget. I'm not willing for them to sacrifice a nourishing dinner for worthless calories.

As mature members of the Body of Christ, we want to continuously empty ourselves. That way, God can fill us *before* God has no choice but to bring us to those dry, desert places to help us see how much we need Him instead of the things of this world. In the same way, there's a difference between emptying yourself and *being emptied.* God will get us to an empty place to fill us because He's a good Father. He wants us filled with the right stuff, and He will help us be empty—but it's more difficult when we are being *emptied* than if we willingly empty ourselves. Emptying ourselves is something we learn—we learn to cultivate a hunger for God rather than filling up on whatever junk is handy.

We live in a culture of instant gratification. Hungry? Go through a drive-through. Tired? Energy drink. Lonely? Swipe right on the app. But as you've probably learned, there's a world of difference between the quality of a home-cooked meal, a good night's rest, an intimate, meaningful relationship, and the quick fix.

God wants His children to learn to be patient and persistent in pursuing Him and be willing to lay down our attempts at control and wait on Him and His timing. Yet, all too often, we want what we want and are even willing to try to control spiritual practices to get it in our timing.

Make Room for God

Fasting is a spiritual discipline where we go without something to make room for God. By its very nature, we're waiting on God. Yet God's people have tried to use fasting incorrectly. Look at how Isaiah addresses God's grievances with His people:

Yet they act so pious! They come to the Temple every day and seem delighted to learn all about me. They act like a righteous nation that would never abandon the laws of its God. They ask me to take action on their behalf, pretending they want to be near me. "We have fasted before you!" they say. "Why aren't you impressed? We have been very hard on ourselves, and you don't even notice it!" "I will tell you why!" I respond. "It's because you are fasting to please yourselves."

Isaiah 58:2-3 (NLT)

I see people fast to get what they want when they want it. They might say, "I want a raise—I'm going to fast until God gives it to me," or, "I need my spouse healed. I'm going to fast 'til God does it." When people do it like this, trying to force God's hand, it's manipulative, fleshly, and twisted by the enemy because it's trying to force God to react to something we're doing on our timing. If something happens, we'll take credit for it. "God did it because *I* fasted," we'll think. But the Bible clearly tells us that it's not by works, lest anyone should boast.

> **FASTING IS EMPTYING OURSELVES SO THAT WE *NO LONGER HAVE CONTROL*.**

In contrast, emptying ourselves is staying hungry and trusting in the power and presence of God, not trying to manipulate Him into working out our situation for us. It's humble and reverent. If called, we fast and pair our physical hunger with spiritual hunger, but it's not to try strong-arming God—it's in response to Him. Fasting is emptying ourselves so that we *no longer have control.*

God is telling us that when we learn how to press into Him, forget ourselves, and start praying by His Spirit for Him to pour into us, letting Him lead, He will spring forth in our lives. But it won't happen until we surrender control of our emptying.

The purpose of fasting is to break your control and authority over your life in a place where you feel empty. It's a posture before God that

says, "I surrender control to you. I'd rather be hungry than fill up with things that aren't of You."

Our job is to empty. (If He has emptied you—if you're in a dry, desert place—embrace that. Don't try to fill it with riches.) God's job is to fill you with His presence. He desires to fill us with His empowering presence! But we must take a lesson from the believers in Acts because they didn't just sit there full; they poured out.

We're gluttonous when we try to get full, control what goes in, and never pour anything out—dangerous to drink because we've become toxic. That's how we end up full . . . but *deadly*.

There must be a stream pouring in and a stream flowing out. When we're empty, God can pour in, and then we, in turn, pour out so He can fill us again.

It's time to stop trying to take control and self-medicate with the things of this world, trying to satisfy ourselves with junk. We have to break self-fulfillment. Instead, God desires a people who will cultivate emptiness and remain hungry until He brings His presence. In the next chapter, let's see what that looked like in Jesus' ministry because it has much to teach us about our lives.

CHAPTER 14:

REMAIN HUNGRY

WE'VE SEEN THAT THE WORLD'S RICHES can never satisfy the hunger God puts in us for Him. When God brings us to the dry, desert places, showing us our emptiness, we have a choice: try to take control and fill ourselves up on the things of this world or allow that emptiness to draw us to Him. If we surrender control and press into Him, He will fill us up and empower us with His Holy Spirit, which is the only thing that will truly satisfy the deep hunger of our souls.

We will pursue God to get our needs met, but will we pursue Him to the level *He* desires? And how do we stay hungry for God, especially in the Western world, where we have so much at our disposal?

In this chapter, I want to look at an event in Jesus' ministry so we can learn these answers straight from Him. A story from Scripture stood out to me because of the incredible move of God released by His people's hunger.

In the Gospel of Matthew, we read about Jesus walking along the Sea of Galilee and climbing up a mountain as people gather with Him. It says,

Then great multitudes came to Him, having with them the lame, blind, mute, maimed, and many others; and they laid them down at Jesus' feet, and He healed them. So the multitude marveled when they saw the mute speaking, the maimed made whole, the lame walking, and the blind seeing; and they glorified the God of Israel.

Matthew 15:30-31

So, Jesus had a powerful healing service, meeting the needs of those who came before Him. Just picture it: thousands of people bringing many who were sick. They were the hopeless, the broken, the desperate. They came to get their needs met because they heard that a Man of God was doing great miracles, and they needed a move of God in their lives.

And He met them there in their need. How long did it take Jesus to move through this gathering crowd, healing people as their loved ones brought them to Him? Let's read on and find out. It says, *"Now Jesus called His disciples to Himself and said, 'I have compassion on the multitude, because they have now continued with Me **three days** and have nothing to eat. And I do not want to send them away hungry, lest they faint on the way'"* (Matthew 15:32, emphasis mine).

Talk about a healing service! Three days sounds like a revival! These people stayed with Jesus as He healed and restored the sick. It says so much about our Savior that He didn't just meet their obvious need; He had compassion on them and understood the cost of their persistence. So, let's see what He did about it.

Then His disciples said to Him, "Where could we get enough bread in the wilderness to fill such a great multitude?" Jesus said to them, "How many loaves do you have?" And they said, "Seven, and a few little fish." So He commanded the multitude to sit down on the ground. And He took the seven loaves and the fish and gave thanks, broke them and gave them to His disciples;

and the disciples gave to the multitude. So they all ate and were filled, and they took up seven large baskets full of the fragments that were left. Now those who ate were four thousand men, besides women and children.

Matthew 15:33-38

Church folks often only pursue God to the level they need, but most won't pursue Him to the level *He* desires. Jesus had a reason to separate the healing service from the feeding service—the feeding service happened *because* the people had remained with Jesus for three days during the healings while they'd demonstrated true hunger.

Out of God's good nature and love for His people, Jesus touched and healed their infirmities. Simply because they were in God's presence, it was a given that He would heal them. But Jesus was moved with *compassion* when He encountered their *hunger*. So, how do we move past only pursuing Him to the level of our need and instead pursue God to the level *He* desires? Let's look at what this text has to teach us about staying hungry.

Move Into the Supernatural

So, the first passage we looked at in this chapter talks about what they brought to God—the lame, the blind, the mute, and others. The text makes it seem like it wasn't even a big deal for Jesus to heal the people. It was more like a given that Jesus would restore them.

We get so caught up in healing that often, we don't move past wanting the stuff *of* God and experience what *God* wants for *us*. If a healing service broke out in church, we'd shout, praise, and go home, happy with leaving it there. We got our needs met, right?

But if we stop there, we never tap into what *God* needs. Do you think it's a lousy doctrine to say God needs something?

I'll tell you what He needs: for us to remain hungry so He can do above and beyond our expectations! If we stop with our met needs, we'll never experience this: *"Now to Him who is able to do exceedingly abundantly above all that we ask or think, according to the power that works in us"* (Ephesians 3:20).

Jesus touched these hungry people and healed them because that's just who God is, but notice it says that Jesus was moved to compassion when they remained hungry. The word "compassion" here in this scripture means deeply moved or affected. I don't know about you, but I want to be someone who deeply moves and affects God. Don't you want to be someone who causes God to get off His throne because your hunger and pursuit move Him?

It's one thing when we lay our problems at His feet, and God doesn't even have to move; He touches and heals you because that's just who He is. It's another when we stay hungry in His presence, affecting Him and moving Him.

I hope that you will not settle for simply getting needs met but that you will move past wanting things from God and into affecting God with your hunger for Him. That, my friends, is where the supernatural really begins to happen!

We've equated the supernatural with healing, but God created our bodies to heal themselves. Just watch as you get a cut; the bleeding stops, and then, in time, the wound heals. Let me mess up your religious thinking: We shouldn't get so excited when bodies are healed. We appreciate and honor God for it, but this is just God being Himself. He built us to heal, but when Jesus gets involved, sometimes He manifests the process quickly, which is a miracle. But I want to propose to you that the real supernatural move of God hasn't even taken place yet if we're still just talking about healing. God has something powerful waiting for us on the other side of our hunger.

Supernatural Multiplication

The text tells us that there were four thousand men, in addition to all the women and children, so we're probably talking about four thousand families. Some estimates place the actual number between fifteen and twenty-five thousand people! Four thousand is incredible enough, but as many as twenty-five thousand blows me away even more!

Jesus supernaturally multiplied the loaves and fish when hungry people moved God. If we want to see God move the way *He* wants to, we need to press into our hunger to the point it affects God and not just us. We want to affect the Earth, but God wants us to impact Heaven! We often only think of the physical, but God is interested in the Kingdom.

God put us on this planet to influence the world for Him, but the church is not to be a social club—we are to point people to Heaven. We already affect the Earth by just being here, but those willing to empty themselves and stay hungry will move Heaven and show people the true nature of our loving Father.

How many of us would pursue God for three days with Jesus as He healed the sick and we grew increasingly hungry? Some people get mad if the service goes over an hour! These people persisted. I wonder how many prayers we would see answered with supernatural multiplication if we pursued God with the hunger these people had. Sometimes, our prayers are answered the way we want because it's our timing, and sometimes, God's answer is no. But how often are we praying out of *want* instead of hunger for God? Are we hungry to see God move *His* way?

Jesus didn't want to send the people away until they were full, and I want to learn to pray past my needs until God is moved to supernatural multiplication. Jesus was moved with compassion because these people remained hungry, and I want that for myself and you as well.

Wait on God

Matthew 15:32 says the people *"have now continued"* three days, meaning they abided or waited. This makes me think of the famous passage in Isaiah 40:31, which says, *"But those who wait on the Lord shall renew their strength; they shall mount up with wings like eagles, they shall run and not be weary, they shall walk and not faint."* Jesus fulfilled this scripture in their midst, renewing their strength so they would not faint because they waited on Jesus hungry.

We like this scripture for people who are in their broken moments. But "waiting on the Lord" is not just for a bad day at work or an argument with your spouse—it's waiting while broken. It's remaining empty.

How long will you wait, broken and empty, on God? How long will you remain in that place and still pursue Him even when nothing is going right, even when you're tempted to take control and try to fill that emptiness with something—with *anything* that might take the ache away?

I lived this in the dry desert time before my wife and I founded our church, waiting on the Lord as He quietly did something that I could not perceive. It was one of the most challenging times in my life . . . but it was completely worth it. I've been in it again—a long journey—as I've gone through this health battle.

Those who *wait* will not grow weary and faint. Those who don't leave Him when He fixes their problem are the ones who mount up with wings like eagles! Getting our needs met and our problems fixed should not satisfy our hunger because so much more awaits us on the other side of our needs.

I want you to see that people were healed that day, but many thousands ate from almost nothing. The miracle wasn't the healing; it was the feeding. The modern church would be satisfied with a healing service, but I believe these people were *healed* because they were *hungry*. They waited on God, pressing in, for days—and they were renewed.

God loves it when we want Him and when our pursuit in affliction provokes a mighty supernatural outpouring that releases Heaven's overflow.

In John 10:10, Jesus says, *"I have come that they may have life and that they may have it* more abundantly." Don't stop short of *abundant* life overflow because you only pursue God to the level of your need! Pursue God until *He* is satisfied—until His supernatural multiplication changes everything!

In Matthew 15:29-31, the people had an expectation of what God could do for them, which is why they brought the sick to Jesus. They believed the Lord was their healer. However, they couldn't even imagine the supernatural power Jesus would display in verses 32-38.

We can't even dream of what God wants to do! We read in 1 Corinthians 2:9, *"Eye has not seen, nor ear heard, nor have entered into the heart of man the things which God has prepared for those who love Him."* To which I'd like to add: to those who wait on the Lord and remain hungry.

Are You Hungry?

We often ask people, "What are you expecting from God?" But there's a higher level because our expectation often only meets our needs. A better question is: "Are you *hungry*?" If you're hungry for a deeper relationship and to see what *God* wants to be fulfilled, you'll move far past your met need and begin to release the overflow of Heaven.

BUT HUNGRY PEOPLE LIVE IN PREPARATION FOR WHAT GOD WANTS.

I'm hungry for what I cannot even know or imagine! I want Heaven to get

involved in Earth things and to change the world in ways I can't even fathom! Don't you?

Hurting people live in expectation for what they want. But hungry people live in preparation for what *God* wants. Why did four thousand families eat and were filled? Jesus had healed their hurts, and their hunger prepared them for what *He* had for them rather than just what *they* wanted. The fact there were just seven loaves of bread, and fish didn't shake Jesus because their hunger had already moved Him. Four thousand families ate because four thousand were hungry.

We pray for increase, overflow, and the Kingdom to expand, but do our prayers match our hunger? God will pour out according to our hunger level because Heaven ignores the conditions and limitations of the Earth and moves as God ordains. What the limits are in humanity or what's happening here on Earth makes no difference—the spirit realm is more real than what we see. Heaven overflows with abundance, so we can't measure what God will do with the little bit we bring Him—our "loaves and fishes."

God isn't limited to what you see. Your hunger moves Him! If you get hungry for more of God's presence, He will blow your mind! He isn't limited by how much you bring Him. He can do even more with *less*! I'm convinced that if they had not brought Jesus seven loaves of bread and a few little fish, Jesus would have begun making them appear out of nowhere simply because people remained hungry and waited on God. He wants us empty because then He can show off His goodness!

If you empty yourself, God will move Heaven, Hell, and Earth to satisfy your hunger for Him! Jesus could feed four thousand families with a couple of fish and some bread. What does He want to do through your emptiness?

God touched every person in that crowd of perhaps twenty-thousand people with His presence—not one was left out. We have over eight billion people in the world now upon whom God wants to pour out greater grace. He wants to do something we've never seen before, and He's waiting for you and me to get empty and stay hungry for Him so He can show up and show off.

The level of our hunger determines the size of our meal. If you want a snack, go to the convenience store. But if you want an all-you-can-eat buffet, you must go to the right place! God is ready to serve you the spiritual meal of a lifetime, but His Spirit gives according to *your* spirit's hunger. The miracle on the side of a mountain where Jesus fed over twenty-thousand people, was necessitated by hunger. Jesus would not send them away hungry. He did not set out with plans for a massive fish fry, but their demand required a response from Jesus and created the recipe for the miraculous.

So, are you hungry?

Are you ready to quit being satisfied by anything less than what God wants? Are you ready to live empty so that your hunger places a demand on the Spirit of God? If you're willing to quit filling up on the worthless things of this world, God has incredible blessings to pour out on everyone empty enough to receive Him.

He *wants* to move! Your hunger moves Him—so don't be satisfied with anything less than His best for you!

Many of us don't even know what that kind of hunger looks like. We have settled for trying to get our needs met when God has spiritual multiplication in mind that would blow us away.

If you want that, pray this prayer with me: "God, I don't know if I've ever been that hungry before. I don't know how to get there on my own. All I know is that I want to live hungry for more of Your presence. Teach me how to empty myself and remain hungry, waiting on You to pour out like You never have before!"

Currently, countless people are hungry and don't even know what they're hungry for. The world hasn't satisfied them, and while people

in the church have filled up on religious things, God is ready to fill the multitudes with His presence. He is looking for those who will stand up and demonstrate how to direct their hunger to the only One who can satisfy them.

Will you stay hungry until He moves?

CHAPTER 15:
PREPARE THE RIGHT WAY

IN THE PREVIOUS CHAPTERS, we saw the importance of entering empty and remaining hungry for God, even after our needs are met. We witnessed that Jesus was moved with compassion after the people remained with Him, and after the need-meeting of healing. That's when spiritual multiplication happened, and thousands of men, women, and children ate miraculously from just a few loaves and fish. The power of Heaven responded to their hunger.

We find many "if" and "then" statements in Scripture. These are promises God makes based on our obedience. A famous one is in 2 Chronicles 7:14, which says, *"If My people who are called by My name will humble themselves, and pray and seek My face, and turn from their wicked ways, then I will hear from heaven, and will forgive their sin and heal their land."*

But before the Lord told Israel that, He put it on David's heart that it wasn't right for him to build a house for himself without building one for the Ark of God. I want to look at a powerful passage that shows how God desires us to leave this world's concerns behind. If we do so, forgetting what people think of us and living only to please God, He has a beautiful promise for us to experience.

You see, we do not empty ourselves by the standards of what's popular and easy. Culture is almost always going to say something different than God is. We empty ourselves according to the Word of God and the passions He puts on our hearts, much like King David did.

A Man After God's Own Heart

King Saul was the first man Samuel anointed king of Israel. He was a good-looking guy, taller than everyone else, and a great warrior. Shy at first, Saul had many victories over the enemies of God's people. But soon, something began to happen. Saul got caught up in his own successes, began going his own way, and disobeyed God to do what *seemed* spiritual but was, in fact, based on fear. Samuel told Saul to wait seven days until he came to Gilgal to offer up a sacrifice. When Samuel did not come in seven days, Saul took it upon himself to make an offering. He was not willing to wait on the Lord. He was not willing to remain empty but was so selfishly driven to satisfy his own desires, that he took it upon himself to attempt to force advancement, a move of God, without the presence of God cultivated through obedience.

Saul revealed his heart after only a short time as king by offering the burnt offering without Samuel the prophet when he saw his soldiers scattering. He feared God wouldn't be able to do it if too many soldiers left. He took matters into his own hands, and no sooner was he done offering the sacrifice himself than Samuel arrived and saw what he'd done. Saul continued to coast for many years as king, with one of the final straws that he and the people kept the spoils of war that should've been offered as a firstfruit to God. (Remember how important the first is to God!)

Because Saul's heart no longer followed God but his desires and fears, Samuel prophesied that the Lord would seek a man after His own heart. We read, *"And when He had removed him* [Saul], *He raised up for them David as king, to whom also He gave testimony and said, 'I have found David the son of Jesse, a man after My own heart, who will do all My will'"* (Acts 13:22).

David was not perfect; in fact, he made some incredible mistakes and sinned in ways we would say disqualified him. But David wasn't a man after God's own heart because he was perfect. He was willing to be corrected by God. David learned to repent. God could touch Him, and He wanted to be touched by God. He remained pliable, and God could shape Him. Because He was submitted to the Father, the Father could pour Himself into him. In Psalm 51, David wrote that he had discovered God did not want sacrifices. Instead, you might remember that he noted, *"The sacrifices of God are a broken spirit, a broken and a contrite heart—these, O God, You will not despise"* (Psalm 51:17).

However, David had an important lesson to learn about entering empty and not regarding people's opinions.

Are You Preparing Before God or Men?

In 1 Chronicles 13, we read that King David consulted with all the leaders of the people—he looked to them first, before God. This is never a good way to start.

Then David consulted with the captains of thousands and hundreds, and with every leader. And David said to all the assembly of Israel, "If it seems good to you, and if it is of the Lord our God, let us send out to our brethren everywhere who are left in all the land of Israel, and with them to the priests and Levites who are in their cities and their common-lands, that they may gather together to us; and let us bring the ark of our God back to us, for we have not inquired at it since the days of

Saul." Then all the assembly said that they would do so, for the thing was right in the eyes of all the people.

1 Chronicles 13:1-4

Notice how David put what the leaders thought ahead of God? We have done this in the church, but while we've sought a move of God, we've paid our first attention to the thoughts of men.

The Ark of the Covenant was the mobile special place of God's presence before Jesus came and restored the connection between God and people. It represented and housed God's presence, and even Israel's enemies learned to respect God because of it. David wanted to bring it into Jerusalem, but he started off on the wrong foot.

David sought a move of God, but we're about to see he prepared in man's presence. Priests were to carry the Ark on long poles. The priests had famously carried it before the people when they walked across the flood-swollen Jordan River in Joshua 3. Still, David didn't understand that God had a way of doing things, and his missed opportunity would leave him angry.

TOO MANY LEAN ON CHARISMA AND NOT CHRIST. THEY VALUE GIFTEDNESS OVER OILINESS.

We read, *"So they carried the ark of God on a new cart from the house of Abinadab, and Uzza and Ahio drove the cart. Then David and all Israel played music before God with all their might, with singing, on harps, on stringed instruments, on tambourines, on cymbals, and with trumpets"* (1 Chronicles 13:7-8).

God's presence was never meant to be carried on a cart pulled by cows any more than our churches were meant to be filled with many of the activities we have today. A "new cart" might look like a new program, system, leader, stage design, branding, or song. We try to provoke God into acting by attempting something new, but if it isn't according to His word or led by His Spirit, none of these things matter.

We don't even know who Uzza and Ahio were. Were they priests? All we know for sure is that they were Abinadab's sons. In the church, it seems as though we are trusting leaders to bring people into the presence of God because of proximity. They're gifted communicators; that doesn't mean they're anointed. Too many lean on charisma and not Christ. They value giftedness over oiliness. I am living proof that a gift doesn't matter. If I'm anointed, I won't have to carry the weight and the burden of preparing something profound that tries to elicit a response; instead, I will have rivers of living water flowing out of me.

David and the people were having a church service. Yet, while the people played music with all their might, I feel it's telling it was *their might*. While all of Israel played, they were playing to produce something. They were in performance, attracting attention, and seeking to create a move of God separate from the way God moves. So they were trying to wax full.

The Bible says, *"'Not by might nor by power, but by My Spirit,' says the Lord of hosts."* I love good worship music, but how much of it is by God's Spirit, and how much of it is just "with all our might"? We sing many songs that are void of biblical truth but heavy on charisma. They play on emotional response instead of an "emptying" response. It is an avenue the enemy knows well. Wouldn't it make sense that the former worship leader of Heaven is still in the business of writing church "worship songs" that are absent of biblical truth and heavy on self-gratification? We keep trying to figure out what will cause God to move, and we fill up with so many things when only one thing matters—the presence of God.

When we put anything ahead of the presence of God, we're going to have problems, and sometimes, it will take something extreme to get our attention. We read on,

> *And when they came to Chidon's threshing floor, Uzza put out his hand to hold the ark, for the oxen stumbled. Then the anger of the Lord was aroused against Uzza, and He struck him because he put his hand to the ark; and he died there before God. And David became angry because of the Lord's outbreak against Uzza; therefore that place is called Perez Uzza to this day. David was afraid of God that day, saying, "How can I bring the ark of God to me?"*

1 Chronicles 13:9-12

A threshing floor is where they sifted wheat; they would knock it around until it broke down into the wheat and the chaff. It was here that things broke down for David's first attempt to bring the Ark to Jerusalem, and it cost someone his *life*.

God was trying to get their attention! We mistakenly think God will respect our efforts if we do something with all our might. A good thing will never replace the *right* thing. We can't fill up on all the things of this world and believe that we're going to please God our way when He has made a way for us to experience His presence.

Thank God, I don't know anyone who has been struck dead lately. But some of us have broken down and blamed the devil. We can accuse the devil when he's not even around, when it's something that God allowed, and happened because *we* were out of order. It's not because we're under attack; it's because we've entered rebellion, trying to do it our way. When we attempt to do it our way, sooner or later, it's going to break down.

You may have been doing it with all your might when all hell broke loose in your life, but perhaps this is your wake-up call that things are out of order. The Ark would not have almost fallen if the priests

carried it, as God had commanded. Instead, a man died because a cow fell. God is trying to wake us up today, and while the enemy stays in a constant posture of attack, it should not matter to the Body of Christ. Let's not be so aware of what the enemy is doing; instead, let's be mindful of what God is doing!

In this passage, nobody's approach or ways changed until someone died! Things must die in our lives, too, and they're our wrong attitudes, perspectives, ways, and mindsets. If you are in a dry, desert place, feel as though everything is crumbling around you, and are desperate to see change, it is time to embrace what God may be doing with a contrite and broken heart.

Who Is God to You?

David, a man after God's own heart, hadn't shifted to Psalm 51 yet. Instead, these events made him angry. David got mad at God, the very thing he was after. Why? Because he was embarrassed. He was ashamed because while he gave lip service to God, something else had become God to him: people's opinions.

Remember how this all started—before David consulted God, he got people's opinions. What would they think when he wasn't able to bring the Ark into Jerusalem, and it cost someone his life?

SENT PEOPLE HAVE AN AUDIENCE OF ONE.

David called the Lord "God," but the attention and desires of the people had become a god to him. David was on the brink of becoming the person he despised, the failed king, Saul. Saul once had an anointing on his life, too, to be God's man and king. Yet when he felt the pressures of people's desire and got too impressed with his accomplishments, these things took over Saul's ego to the point where he no longer would wait on the Lord. He was hungrier to be praised by people as a great leader than he was for God, and the same fate threatened to happen to David. It's possible that David's line and kingship hung in the balance. Sent people have an audience of One.

It doesn't make any difference what you call somebody. All that matters is how you position yourself before them. You can call someone a father, but if you don't position yourself as a son, it makes no difference. We can call God our Father and Lord of our lives, but if we give preference to everything else in our lives, causing all the worthless things of this world to be more important than Him, calling Him Lord makes no difference.

We will receive according to the way we posture ourselves. So, do we want to wait on people's opinions, or do we want to wait at the feet of Jesus? Only one of these things really matters. We can either build our lives and our churches on the rock, or we can build them on the shifting sands of opinions and culture.

We will receive from God according to how we position ourselves.

Has God Become an "It" to You?

David wanted the presence of God in Jerusalem, which is good. But he began to prepare the wrong way. In our modern times, it may have looked like asking, "How should we structure our services?" or, "What do you think will make the most people happy with our church?" or, "What do my friends think my dating relationship should look like?" If we are sitting around and talking to people first, any preparation for the presence of God is terminally on the wrong track.

David was a sent leader and was called by God. He was anointed and commissioned, but now, after his victories, the trajectory of his life was being shaped by people's opinions. God had given him an assignment through the Prophet Samuel when no one else believed in David, but now he was deciding how to approach God based on the opinions of the same people who discounted him.

We live under the demand of something. If we are not careful, we will permit ourselves to live under the demands and expectations of people. The enemy will borrow the demands of people in your life to rob you of your Kingdom existence and divine inheritance. It becomes a pressure so great that it destroys you because there was never a grace given to you to live out of the expectations of others. We're to be under the yoke of the Holy Spirit. That yoke is easy, and that burden is light, and with it comes the unforced rhythm of grace to be in an effective and productive co-mission with Jesus.

One tiny word reveals the state of David's heart better than almost anything else. Going back to the passage we started with, let's look for it together: "Let *us bring the ark of our God back to us, for we have not inquired at it since the days of Saul*" (1 Chronicles 13:3). Did you see it?

It's like that children's riddle—the little word is "it." David didn't say, "We have not inquired of *Him*." He said, *"It."* God had become an "it" to David somewhere along the way. No one called him on it, because this was what seemed right *"in the eyes of all the people"* (1 Chronicles 13:4).

Thank God for His mercy! Even though David had given first preference to people's opinions, in His mercy, God still gave David an opportunity. He could stay mad at God, hung up on his embarrassment before those whose opinion he craved, or he could choose to humble himself and become a man of broken and contrite spirit.

I don't know God's calling on your life, but everybody has one. Because of decisions, circumstances, or attitudes, you may feel that opportunity or calling has passed you by. Maybe you're mad at God, embarrassed, or disappointed. But I am here to tell you that under the mercy of God, it is still alive! Your purpose has not been recalled; the

WE, LIKE DAVID, MUST PREPARE DIFFERENTLY.

plan is still in place. Why? Because yours is a part of His greater purpose, and He has guaranteed that His purposes will prevail! You still have a chance! It's never too late as long as you're breathing to make a different decision and choose to humble yourself and be broken by the desert opportunity you're in.

We, like David, must prepare differently. We must stop making our own plans and seeking people's opinions first because that will only leave us angry and bitter when everything we try to do in God's name fails. David's attempt to bring the Ark of the Covenant to Jerusalem left a man dead, but if we prepare the right way, God has an amazing promise in store for us.

My friend, if we will lay aside our own ways, the opinions of people, and the worthless filler of this world, God wants to fill our empty vessels with His presence!

After this traumatic experience, David shifted his perspective. In the next chapter, we will see that David laid aside his concern about people's opinions to pursue God recklessly! And when we look at it, I believe you will see the power God wants to pour out if we are willing to uncover ourselves to embrace Him fully.

CHAPTER 16:
UNCOVER YOURSELF

IN THE PREVIOUS CHAPTER, we saw that David had made people's opinion a god to him while the Lord who made him king had become an "it." David got mad at God when his preparations before men backfired, and Uzza paid the price with his life. His death was a dramatic wake-up call for David.

We typically think of the cross bringing resurrection life, but it may shock you to realize that it killed something, too. The cross was so powerful and miraculous because we have absolutely no ability to control, rescue, or make ourselves right with God. The old man inside each of us had to die; it couldn't just be tweaked or refined. God had to *kill* the sinful nature in us. For God to have room in our lives, something had to come out of our vessels, so God killed all the sin, the fallen nature, and the control the flesh had on us.

With the old you dead, a new you could be brought to life by the Holy Spirit. Paul writes that we who are in Christ are new creations (2 Corinthians 5:17), that our old man was crucified with Christ (Romans 6:5-11), and that it is no longer we who live, but Christ who lives within us (Galatians 2:20). Then he gives us this instruction: *"That you put*

off, concerning your former conduct, the old man which grows corrupt according to the deceitful lusts, and be renewed in the spirit of your mind, and that you put on the new man which was created according to God, in true righteousness and holiness." (Ephesians 4:22-24).

This "put off" is an action—one David would learn as we go back to the story of how he brought the Ark of the Covenant to Jerusalem. Throughout this book, I've been trying to show you that if we want a great move of God, we must empty ourselves of the worthless things of this world. That is this "putting off"—it's our responsibility in the sanctification process as we put the things of the flesh to death and embrace new life in Christ. We can preach, shout, and run around our churches, but the Spirit only works through those who will give themselves to God as empty vessels.

Jesus died for us so that we might live, but now it is our turn to put off the old man and this world so that we can live for Christ. We can give our lives daily, pour ourselves out as a drink offering, and accept the weight and responsibility that God has set before us. If we don't accept this responsibility to make room for Him in our lives, the world will never see Him. They may see the baggage of the church, but God pours out on people through empty vessels, and it's my greatest desire to see you and I learn to be those believers who don't hold onto our old lives but willingly pour them out for God.

Let's pick back up with David's story to see how he realized this and the state of reckless, abandoned worship that it brought him.

Prepare the Right Way

In the previous chapter, we saw that when David started by consulting with the people rather than God first, it got his whole venture off on the wrong foot. But in the aftermath of this disaster, David began to prepare the right way. We pick up the story a few months after David's first failed attempt:

David built houses for himself in the City of David; and he prepared a place for the ark of God, and pitched a tent for it. Then David said, "No one may carry the ark of God but the Levites, for the Lord has chosen them to carry the ark of God and to minister before Him forever." And David gathered all Israel together at Jerusalem, to bring up the ark of the Lord to its place, which he had prepared for it.

1 Chronicles 15:1-3

We read that David built a place for the Ark. The word "place" here means "home." I love the figurative translation of the word "place." It means "the condition of the body and mind." David, instead of looking outward, prepared inward. He had to reassess his mindset. Uzza died because he didn't prepare for the presence of God but instead prepared before the opinion of people. David was doing it differently this time.

Because of God's mercy, David could self-reflect and examine his mindset. If we learn this principle for ourselves, we could change the world! Many of our churches have done the same thing David did and put people's opinions before God, but if we reassess our mindsets, God can begin to do transformative work through the power of His Holy Spirit.

The children of Israel housed the Ark of the Covenant in a tabernacle or tent for many years. David prepared by pitching a tent for the Ark of God. The word for "pitch" here means "to stretch." The word "tent" means "a meeting place or dwelling." We know that if our earthly bodies, which Paul likens to tents, are destroyed, our real home is eternal in Heaven. So, as David pitched a tent for the Ark of the Covenant, he was also stretching himself out in surrender before God.

Everything begins to shift when you obey God when He tells you to stretch yourself out, surrender before Him, and "pitch your tent" before the Lord. This kind of surrendered life means to empty ourselves before the Lord, and when we do this, we're preparing the *right* way.

David called for the priests to get ready as well.

*He said to them, "You are the heads of the fathers' houses of the Levites; sanctify yourselves, you and your brethren, that you may bring up the ark of the Lord God of Israel to the place I have **prepared** for it. For because you did not do it the first time, the Lord our God broke out against us, because we did not consult Him about the proper order." So the priests and the Levites sanctified themselves to bring up the ark of the Lord God of Israel. And the children of the Levites bore the ark of God on their shoulders, by its poles, as Moses had commanded according to the word of the Lord.*

1 Chronicles 15:12-15 (emphasis mine)

We partner with the drawing and conviction of the Holy Spirit in the sanctification of our lives. Still, David's instruction to the priests to sanctify themselves carries a powerful lesson for us today—the same lesson I've been trying to share throughout the book: emptying ourselves. It's us taking responsibility for choosing what we want more in our lives, the worthless things of this world or the presence of God. The Spirit sanctifies us, but we choose what we will be filled with daily. As we've seen, this is a prerequisite for God pouring out His presence.

Because Jesus' finished work on the cross was not our responsibility, we tend to put all responsibility for Kingdom work on the cross. We somehow think that Jesus will work it all out without us lifting a finger. And while we never want to step out ahead of Him without preparing for the presence of God, we bear the responsibility for being His hands and feet on the Earth. Works do not save us, but James showed us that we demonstrate our faith through our good works, obeying the Word, and "sanctifying ourselves" by choosing to empty ourselves.

Plan for His Presence

The word "prepared" stuck out to me in this passage. We do a lot of planning in our lives and our businesses. Proverbs tells us, *"There are many plans in a man's heart, nevertheless the Lord's counsel—that will stand"* (19:21). But for all of our plans, we often prepare poorly spiritually. Everything in the natural realm is a reflection of the spiritual realm, and while it is popular to have missions and vision statements in our churches, we have poorly prepared to host the presence of God. We can plan things by ourselves without God, but we cannot prepare for His presence without consulting Him.

When David first consulted with the people, his mission was already a failure. After a mindset shift, he was able to make plans consulting with God rather than people. Authentic preparation always involves consulting the Lord *first*.

If we don't consult God first, we turn to things like people and culture and make our plans according to what's popular and easy. The "popular" church is ineffective and only scratches the surface. It's full of broken and directionless people with trust issues looking for radical life change in all the wrong places. Instead of consulting culture, let's instead consult Father God!

As with David, we find ourselves at a destiny decision and with the opportunity to bring the presence of the Lord to a nation. David found himself at this crossroads because he had missed an opportunity months before. Thanks to the mercy of God, David (like the church) still has the chance to usher in the presence of God by being an empty vessel. Let's avoid making the same mistake again!

OPPORTUNITIES OF A LIFETIME ARE ONLY AVAILABLE IN THE LIFETIME OF THE OPPORTUNITY!

David failed the first time because he prepared in the presence of people instead of God. He got another opportunity, but we do not know what tomorrow will bring. How many opportunities will we have to usher in God's presence? He's constantly presenting us with open doors, opportunities, connections, and people, but we never know how many chances we will have. Opportunities of a lifetime are only available in the lifetime of the opportunity!

I don't want to miss the moments God places before me! I want to be ready when He gives me the opening. Every opportunity we get is because God created the possibility for connection. Even the clothes on our backs are good gifts permitted by God. As a body, we have the opportunity to bring the presence of God to our nation, so let's stop taking our mission for granted and missing the opportunities He presents us.

I grew up with everybody expecting a move of God every Sunday. Sometimes we saw a move, but I'm not sure it was always God! I can't say it was always God with clarity because some people can say the right things and do the right actions without the right heart or preparation. I wonder if they were empty vessels or if something was still left in the bottom, like the dirty water pots when Jesus made water into wine. It's so important for us to prepare properly because we cannot host God in unholy places! Those old pots need to be empty and clean.

We may complain that we have served, prayed, given, sang, shouted, and fellowshipped in His name. But these are just religious activities until we consult God and prepare our hearts and attitudes for His desires. This might offend some religious people, but read Jesus' words: *"Many will say to Me in that day, 'Lord, Lord, have we not prophesied in Your name, cast out demons in Your name, and done many wonders in Your name?' And then I will declare to them, 'I never knew you; depart from Me, you who practice lawlessness!'"* (Matthew 7:22-23). Until we consult God and prepare our hearts and attitudes, we are not prepared for the presence of God.

God had to get David's attention because he was trying to host God's presence in an unholy way. Uzza died for it, and I wonder how many churches have, too. How many people are dying around us because presence isn't our pursuit, and His righteousness is not our priority? But David received the correction and planned the right way by making a home for the presence of God. Let's read on to see how he'd changed.

Surrender the Throne

When David saw that God had blessed Obed-Edom, who had cared for the Ark after David's first attempt to bring it to Jerusalem, he brought God's tangible presence home with gladness and a great celebration. But this time, he did it the right way.

I love a key part of the scripture here: *"And so it was, when God helped the Levites who bore the ark of the covenant of the Lord, that they offered seven bulls and seven rams"* (1 Chronicles 15:26). Notice first of all that the Levites were carrying the Ark. But even more importantly, *God helped them*, strengthening them so they didn't need a cart! We often think it will be too hard to do it God's way, but that is the lesson—if we do it His way, He helps us!

The same people were present the second time, but David's preparation had shifted the whole environment this time. The change happened because David stopped looking outside (at people) and began to stretch himself inwardly (toward God). The first time, David became angry because of his poor preparation; this time, he had joy in the preparation.

Now, let's switch to the account of this event found in 2 Samuel 6 because I want to draw out a few details. As God was strengthening the Levites to bear the Ark, David was overcome with joy. We read, *"Then David danced before the Lord with all his might; and David was wearing a linen ephod. So David and all the house of Israel*

brought up the ark of the Lord with shouting and with the sound of the trumpet" (2 Samuel 6:14-15). David laid aside all his kingly accessories—his crown, his robe, his jewelry—and he danced before God in only a priestly garment. He emptied himself of any identity outside of the grace of God. David rejected his own glory. He denied a man-made image. He put off how he was publicly viewed to return to how he was first viewed by God: empty, as a child seeking the attention of the Father.

This is a fantastic picture of emptying ourselves! It is an example of how to come before God in broken surrender, over pittance, and recognizing that no title, position, or anything else means anything in the presence of the Almighty. If you stretch yourself out before God's presence, you will find you cannot help but cast your crown at His feet. If you have been the king of your life, it's time to take off your robe, entitlement, and expectations and cast them together with your crown before Jesus in surrender. David was the king, but he didn't let anything about his title or royalty keep him from humbling himself in the presence of Almighty God.

In the Garden of Eden, Adam and Eve were always naked, always unclothed, but *never* uncovered. After they sinned, they were aware. They were outside of God's presence when they were aware of their limitations. Separated from the Spirit, they were subject to their senses. They became more aware, affected, and influenced by the world around them, than the Spirit that had been within them. Outside of being Spirit-led and presence-centered, we become dominated by the very things we were sent to dominate. We assume the responsibility and weight of attempting to control our circumstances by our ability. They thought they could cover themselves before God by sewing fig leaves together, and we've been trying to cover our emptiness ever since. David's "fig leaf" was a crown, a robe, and a title. He hid his brokenness, but God always sees through our attempts to cover ourselves.

To get real and honest before God, David had to eliminate all the symbols that come with being king—things God had given him. It's like God told him, "The first thing you need to do is to take off My crown and get rid of My robe because two can't be kings of the same territory. So, who is going to be the real king? Me or you?"

God is asking the same thing of us. Will we stop hiding behind the baggage of our lives? Will we surrender our supposed right to rule, giving Him that crown? Will we stop ineffectively trying to hide our nakedness and brokenness from the Lord (and ourselves)? At some point, every king of the Earth (whether we decide to do it voluntarily or are forced to do it eternally) will join Heaven, take off our crowns, and lay them at His feet in surrender. *"The twenty-four elders fall down before Him who sits on the throne and worship Him who lives forever and ever, and cast their crowns before the throne, saying: 'You are worthy, O Lord, to receive glory and honor and power; for You created all things, and by Your will they exist and were created'"* (Revelation 4:10-11).

David took his opportunity to strip off the robe, crown, and everything else to dress humbly in nothing but a linen priestly ephod. The linen ephod represented the presence of God to the people, and while they thought His presence would come with the Ark, David showed them that God's presence would never come through an Ark if it didn't show up through their king first. This prophetically established the principle for the church that the presence of the Lord and His salvation to our world would not ultimately come through an Ark, or any religious fixture, but it would penetrate the Earth through us.

Usually, only the high priest wore the ephod, but when David pressed into God and heard His heart, he realized the priority wasn't on him being king. It wasn't on the people, the business, or the territory of kingship. The priority was being a priest and leading the people into the presence of God.

David demonstrated that he had learned from his hard earlier lesson. Instead of prioritizing the people's wants or his dignity as king, he showed that he would not lead them into the presence of God as their king first, but as their priest. We need people who care to be aware of His presence and people's need for presence. People who know how to lead others because they understand how to, enter it themselves. We do not need more self-help books, more self-made podcasts, or more self-focused steps to success; we need more selfless people who sense what Heaven desires and know how to be empty enough to vessel it to Earth and how to lead people into it. He made being their spiritual leader the priority.

It is the same for us. Peter writes, *"For you are a chosen people. You are royal priests, a holy nation, God's very own possession. As a result, you can show others the goodness of God, for he called you out of the darkness into his wonderful light"* (1 Peter 2:9 NLT).

We are a kingdom of priests, and if we're willing to strip away every pretense, like David, we can show the way into God's marvelous light to those around us. God is ready to fill those who will lay aside every claim to be the rulers of our lives so that we can instead welcome the King of kings and Lord of lords into His rightful place.

Are you ready to cast aside your robe and crown for an ephod? Are you ready to trade your crown and robe for a linen priestly garment? I am! We will finish this story from David's life in the next chapter because I want to show you how far David has come since his first attempt to bring the presence of God to Jerusalem.

CHAPTER 17:
EVEN MORE

WE HAVE SEEN DAVID learn how to make God the King of his life rather than people's opinions. The first time he tried to bring the Ark of God into Jerusalem, a man lost his life, but now David had prepared the right way for the presence of God and had ushered God's presence into the midst of the people. You'll remember that David danced before the Lord in only a linen ephod, the priestly garment.

But not everyone was pleased with David's abandonment before God. Let's read on to see how he handled people's opinions after pressing into God's presence. *"But as the Ark of the Lord entered the City of David, Michal, the daughter of Saul, looked down from her window. When she saw King David leaping and dancing before the Lord, she was filled with contempt for him"* (2 Samuel 6:16).

After David had the Levites (not a cart) bring the Ark into the special tent he'd made for it, and they'd made the burnt offerings and peace offerings before the Lord, David blessed the people in the Lord's name. They had a party, and everyone, of course, ate great food! But when he got home to bless his family, he didn't get as warm a reception.

His wife, Michal, came out and said, *"How glorious was the king of Israel today, uncovering himself today in the eyes of the maids of*

his servants, as one of the base fellows shamelessly uncovers himself!" (2 Samuel 6:20).

The word "uncovering" means removing. It shows us that David, who was too concerned with people's opinions before, had removed himself from the people's opinions. Michal was still worried about what people thought about appearances and what it would do to David's authority and reputation if people saw him without his crown and robe. Saul's daughter was a princess before David ever became king, and she could not move past this. She could not move past her idea of royalty. Her identity and her entire being were consumed by public perception and her need to be seen and worshiped. The lack of a father leading her to the Father left her in great deficiency.

Today, we're worried about what people will say if we don't keep up appearances in our churches—if we don't keep to a one-hour service, or if the truth might offend someone. Michal's voice is like the devil's, condemning us for prioritizing the presence of God.

But the Holy Spirit is asking you right now what you are willing to do to prepare for His presence. He desires that we empty ourselves of our concerns about what others think. Are you willing to come before God without pretense and to lay your crown at His feet and let Him be the only One on the throne of your life?

Are you willing to uncover yourself, un-busy yourself, and quit hiding yourself from the Father? To be an empty, broken vessel that He can fill?

When the Holy Spirit pours Himself into your willing and waiting vessel, it won't make sense to everyone around you. It won't look like what's popular or even acceptable. If God inspires you to run, dance, and shout, as He did David, will you uncover yourself as a sold-out child of God? Or will you fear people's opinions more than you hunger for the presence of God?

I want to be someone who gets accused of spiritually uncovering myself before the Lord. I don't care what people think because I do it for God and not them. "Look how foolish he is for emptying himself before the presence of people," they may say. I want to be a person of presence! David gave us a great entrance into how to handle this criticism.

Even More Undignified

David's reply to Michal is incredible:

So David said to Michal, "It was before the Lord, who chose me instead of your father and all his house, to appoint me ruler over the people of the Lord, over Israel. Therefore I will play music before the Lord. And I will be even more undignified than this, and will be humble in my own sight. But as for the maidservants of whom you have spoken, by them, I will be held in honor."

2 Samuel 6:21-22

David had stripped away all his pride and ego; he was willing to do anything for the Lord. "If you think this was bad," he was saying, "I just got back in God's presence. You have no idea what it will look like when I'm in the fullness of it!"

The Body of Christ needs leaders who will respond like this to criticism, who aren't as worried about losing someone's tithe check as they are about pleasing God, and who don't underestimate God by making it all about counting stats.

WE NEED PEOPLE OF POWER.

We need people in our churches who are unmistakably surrendered. We need people of power. We cannot be concerned about opinions, critics, and metrics. There are people who are hurting, sick, broken, and lost who need to be healed, delivered, and restored! There are cities and regions that are under such darkness; they need sent people of power! We need men and women like you who respond like David: "I will honor God, no matter how foolish it makes me look!" I want that to be me, and I think if you're still reading, that describes you as well.

When we make it about His presence instead of what people think, we will see the windows of Heaven open and see God change countless lives as He pours out His Spirit! He wants to do a new thing, and we won't be able to keep up with all the people God wants to bring into the wedding feast. From the highways and hedges, God's call is on those who've realized how worthless this world is and who are ready for God's glory to fill their emptiness.

Full, Not Leftovers

We have operated for so long on the leftovers—the little bit of oil and flour left in our cupboards. We've survived on the legacy of faith and the moves of God from the past, but God desires to do a new thing. In the early days of the church, Peter told the crowd this passage had been fulfilled:

> And it shall come to pass in the last days, says God, that I will pour out of My Spirit on all flesh; your sons and your daughters shall prophesy, your young men shall see visions, your old men shall dream dreams. And on My menservants and on My maidservants I will pour out My Spirit in those days; and they shall prophesy.
>
> Acts 2:17-18

If that promise was fulfilled, what does God have for us *now*? It is my fervent prayer that we haven't seen anything yet! The Scripture tells us the latter glory will be greater than that of the past (see Haggai 2:9)! Remember the wedding? He saved the best wine for last! Will we be even more undignified than this, like David?

God has provided a path forward for His church. He called the wedding guests, but the usual suspects didn't come. So, the Lord is inviting any and all who will listen. The wedding feast will be full, and He would not have anyone miss this opportunity!

If your life is full, is it full of God's eternal best for you (His presence), or is it full of things that will not last? God wants a people who are not partly full of the world and partly full of Him but who are wholly-filled with His presence. He doesn't want dirty water pots that still carry the dregs. He yearns for a people who will stay hungry, wait on Him, and settle for nothing less than the outpouring of His Holy Spirit! That leaves you and me with a continual decision—not a one-timer, but a daily call—to empty ourselves and make God the King of our lives.

We have the chance to willingly make the desert times in our lives significant—to lean into them instead of numbing the pain. We have tried everything else to satisfy ourselves with all the things of this world, but nothing will truly satisfy our hunger but Him. He has put a hunger for Heaven in our hearts, but we do not have to wait for eternity to experience His presence. God is ready to pour it, to put the Kingdom of God within you, right now!

I have lived this personally. When I was younger, I filled up on all the wrong things, but they always left me wanting for something more. But through my desert times, especially when launching out as a pastor and later with struggles in my health, God has shown me He is so much more satisfying. Even just waiting on God is better than this world's choicest things!

So, what are *you* hungry for? In your deepest heart, have you realized that nothing else will satisfy you?

If so, you're in the right place. You have clued into one of God's profound secrets. Jesus is the Bread of Life, and He promises that those who come to Him will never hunger and thirst again. We will find He is like a fountain of living water bursting within us. God is just as eager today to fulfill this promise as He was for the children of Israel: *"I am the Lord your God, who brought you out of the land of Egypt; open your mouth wide, and I will fill it"* (Psalm 81:10).

Filled

Whenever His previous moves have run their course, and His people have become hungry again, God has been faithful to make a way. He who poured out of nearly empty jars, provided for His people, and was faithful then and is still faithful today.

He desires to fill us today.

> # HE'S STILL FILLING EMPTY VESSELS.

He cared for widows and orphans, He changed entire countries through the obedience of those who thought they were at death's door, and He filled empty pitchers with the fresh wine of His Spirit. If He has done it before, He'll do it again—and *more.*

He's still filling empty vessels.

Are you willing to pour out the worthless things of this world so that He can fill you up? Are you willing to let yourself be poured out as a drink offering, like Paul, so that God's Spirit can flow to this dry generation?

So many hungry people are just waiting for the next move of God that will change our land! I want to be part of it! And I know you do, too.

Emptying ourselves isn't the end, dear friend; it's the *beginning*. It's the beginning of a great new move of God, and it will be the preparation that sees His presence touch the lives of countless people. He wants to fill you, again and again, with the power of His indescribable presence. He's poised, ready to usher in revival . . .

. . . but only if we Enter Empty.

Author Contact

If you would like to contact Jason Wilson,
find out more information, purchase books,
or request him to speak, please contact:

Jason Wilson

JasonWilson.org

Info@jasonwilson.org

Follow Jason Wilson

Instagram.com/theJasonWilson

facebook.com/pastorjasonwilson

TikTok.com/@jasonwilsonministries

https://www.youtube.com/@JasonWilsonMinistries

About the Author

JASON WILSON is first and foremost a son after the heart of the Father, a husband to Serena, and father to three children, Ashlyn, Braylon, and Cayden.

Spiritually fathered by the late Bishop Tony Miller and mentored by the late Dr. Myles Munroe, Jason is the visionary founder and pastor of Rejuvenate Church, a dynamic, multi-diverse and spirit-filled ministry located in Anderson, South Carolina. Renowned for its authentic surrender, fervent worship, and a passion to be a wellspring of revival, Rejuvenate Church thrives under Jason's leadership, driven by his profound desire to impart into spiritual sons and daughters rooted in the faith and lifestyle of the Kingdom. His mission is to empower believers to become carriers of God's presence, capable of penetrating, and transforming the atmospheres of cities, regions, and nations through an apostolic and prophetic grace.

Jason's leadership is characterized by a unique blend of Spirit-breathed, revelational insight and practical relational teaching. This dual focus allows him to connect any people group with the personal reality of the Kingdom of God, fostering an environment where spiritual growth and personal development go hand in hand. His commitment to fathering leaders extends beyond the pulpit, manifesting in the establishment of the RLA Leadership School. This intensive, two-year program is dedicated to realizing identity and developing capacity in personal, business, and ministry leadership contexts.

With a deep commitment to spiritual growth and leadership development, Jason Wilson continues to make a significant impact through ministry, fathering, and his writing, inspiring countless individuals to pursue a life of divine influence and assignment. Through his apostleship and prophetic leading, he imparts wisdom, power, and spiritual authority, provoking people, leaders, and ministries, to become a move of God in their territories.